W9-CBY-258

Quitter

CLOSING THE GAP BETWEEN YOUR **DAY JOB** & YOUR **DREAM JOB**

Jon Acuff

LAMPO
PRESS
THE LAMPO GROUP, INC.

The opinions and conclusions expressed in this book are those of the
author. All references to websites, blogs, authors, publications, brand names
and/or products are placed there by the author. No recommendation or
endorsement by The Lampo Group, Inc., is intended, nor should any be
implied. Some of the names of people mentioned have been changed to
protect their privacy.

This publication is designed to provide accurate and authoritative
information with regard to the subject matter covered. It is sold with
the understanding that the publisher is not engaged in rendering
financial, accounting or other professional advice. If financial advice or
other expert assistance is required, the services of a competent
professional should be sought.

Editors: Brent Cole and Darcie Clemen
Cover design: Ben Lalisan
Interior design: Mary Hooper, Milkglass Creative

ISBN: 978-0-9829862-7-1

Dedication

"L.E., what should I write for the dedication of my new book?"

L.E., my 7-year-old, "Hmmm, how about, 'To Jenny, L.E., and McRae, the greatest family I could ever have.'?"

"Perfect."

Contents

CHAPTER 1

Don't Quit
Your Day Job

The trick to removing your clothes in a bathroom stall is to start with your shirt. A lot of people will tell you to remove the pants first, but they're wrong. If you go with the shirt, the person in the stall next to you has time to leave the bathroom on his own terms. If you go with the pants first, the pile falling to the ground assaults him. Falling pants one foot from your feet is traumatic at eight in the morning.

Everyone knows to test the door lock before removing any clothing, but lots of people forget the drop test on the door hook. As in, "If I hang my bag and shirt on this, will it drop them to the floor, forcing me to light them on fire in my backyard?" The hook is your best friend because it's nearly impossible to balance something on the metal box that holds the toilet paper.

And let's not even talk about balancing your stuff on the back of the toilet. Asking a toilet to hold your shirt is expecting that piece of porcelain to perform a feat for which it was not designed. The shirt is going to slide off and wedge itself between the toilet and wall. That shirt is gone, and this isn't the Marines. You will leave a man behind. Always choose a stall by the hook strength it offers.

It took me awhile to glean these nuggets of bathroom wisdom. I had to learn by trial and error. You? You've already benefited from my mistakes. Those insights alone are worth the price of this book. But I'm sure you wonder why I have so much experience with stripping in a handicapped stall.

I was doing the reverse Superman.

For a few years I flew all over the country, speaking at weekend conferences. Saving lives, really. Then I would fly home through the night, ride the MARTA train to my office parking lot in Atlanta, grab a pair of khakis from my car, and head to the handicapped stall. No one suspected anything. I would then walk upstairs and disappear into a sea of cubicles, like Clark Kent at the *Daily Planet*.

I hated that.

I hated doing something I loved outside of work, feeling alive and engaged, only to have it all disappear the moment I walked through the door of my day job. I didn't hate the work per se. I liked my boss and the people I worked with. It wasn't that. I just hated that forty hours of my week didn't feel anything like the few hours of my weekend when life made sense.

I hated that my dreams had to go into hibernation every Monday morning. And so, like many other times in my life, I kept coming back to the same thought.

It's quitting time.

The culture of quitters welcomes you

There are two things I am better at than you.

The first is taking off my shoes at airport security. I don't care if you wear flip-flops and fly without a single thread of luggage, I am beating you at this game. I look at the security checkpoint like the corral gate at the rodeo. I consider removing my belt, shoes and laptop similar to the task of a bull rider roping a calf. As soon as I'm done, I throw my hands in the air and breathe in my victory. If I had my way, you'd be allowed to board the plane in the order that you removed your shoes. That would dramatically speed things up.

The other thing I'm better at than you? Quitting jobs. I call scoreboard. My stats speak for themselves.

I held eight jobs in eight years from 1998, when I graduated from college, until 2006. These weren't petty, part-time jobs, like that summer I was a mailman or that afternoon I spent as a carny.

The jobs I quit were 40-hour-a-week, 401(k)-offering, health-insurance–transferring, me-in-a-plain-colored-cubicle jobs. These were career jobs for most of my coworkers, and in a period of twelve years, I managed to quit six of the eight. Another I was fired from and the other went out of business.

I cultivated a high quality of quitting over those years. The first time, I took my boss out to dinner as if we were breaking up. It was amateur. It was also overkill.

At no point should quitting a job involve fondue and soft candlelight. The second time, I was nervous and tossed a quitting grenade into a guy named Derek's office at Staples. I was an interactive copywriter but had been there for an eternity. A year. I saw Derek in his office with another guy named Thom. I approached the doorway and proclaimed, "Derek, I need to give you my two weeks' notice." Thom stared at me. I backed out and returned to my cubicle like I had just told Derek I needed more paper clips.

But by the last time I quit, I didn't have to say a word. My boss looked into my eyes and said, "Wait. Jon, are you quitting?" That's how good I got. No two weeks' notice needed. My dark mocha eyes did all the work.

I used to think I was unique, that perhaps I had a problem with staying at one job for a long time. It turns out I am extremely common. A recent survey revealed that 84 percent of employees plan to look for a new job this year.[1] Furthermore, the average tenure at a job is dramatically changing from generation to generation. A U.S. Department of Labor study revealed that the median tenure for the 55–64-year-old category is 10 years. For the 25–34-year-old category, the average tenure is only 3.1 years. You and I will quit lots and lots of jobs.[2]

Why?

We used to stay at jobs for decades. We got a gold watch for staying at a job for thirty years and then we retired to some flat, sweaty part of Florida to eat dinner at 4:30 in the afternoon. But somewhere along the way that changed.

At some point we stopped being stayers and formed a long line of leavers. We started seeing motion as a sign of success and transition as a sign of progress.

The golden watch has become the other end of golden handcuffs. We now look at steady jobs as less of a goal and more of a necessary evil. They aren't fun; they simply fund our lives. They are cash cows we need but don't want. There's a reason why, at the time of this writing, Tim Ferriss' *The 4-Hour Workweek* is the best-selling career book on Amazon. The idea of only working four hours a week sounds appealing because the general assumption is that work is a terrible way to spend our time. Spending far less time doing something terrible is a pretty terrific proposition.

I think this attitude starts when we're kids but it really kicks into high gear when we're in college. Well-meaning but unthinking adults tell us things like, "Have fun now. Take a semester in Europe. Travel while you can."

People position adulthood like it's the end of your life, not the beginning. You've had your fun. Now it's time to grow up. You've lived it up. Now it's time to start dying.

The prevailing message is to do all the life-giving stuff in your first twenty-one years and then hop aboard the grave train. Apparently when you're thirty, Europe will be closed. They'll check IDs at the Rock of Gibraltar. If you're not in college, you can't go to Italy; you have to vacation in Boynton Beach or Branson, Missouri.

So we get a Euro Rail pass and try to find ourselves while we can. We go skydiving or take a cooking class while we can. We buy an impractical car or volunteer somewhere that speaks to our hearts while we can. All the while we are terrified that the real world is just around the next corner.

That phrase "while you can" is a weird one when you think about it. If you were about to get married, no one would tell you, "Hey, make sure you sleep with a bunch of people while you can. Make sure you spend all your money while you can. Make sure you travel and have fun while you can."

They wouldn't say that because that would be a terribly emo way to describe what marriage can be like. And you'd know it wasn't true because marriage can be fun. You know people who are happily married. You'd be able to uncover the "while you can" lies quickly if they were applied to marriage. Yet for some reason you and I have a hard time recognizing the same lies surrounding our jobs.

We buy into the lie that work is usually miserable.

We buy into the lie that it's possible to separate who we are at work from who we are outside of work.

We buy into the lie that to escape the drudgery, to be the person we want to be all week long, to follow our dream, the first step is to quit our jobs.

It's not.

Despite the fact that quitting your job is the new American dream, it's usually the worst thing you can do right now. Here's why.

The Donnie dilemma

Donnie was the worst boss I ever had. That's not his real name, but there was a bully named Donnie on my school bus when I was a kid. He used to show me the scars on his knuckles from punching kids with braces like me. One afternoon, after we got dropped off from school, he threw my book bag under the rear tires of the bus. It was run over. He might have invented the concept of throwing someone under the bus right there in Hudson, Massachusetts, that day. Either way his name was Donnie, and it's a fitting pseudonym for my worst boss.

He chewed tobacco in the office, and I wasn't working for Major League Baseball. I worked at a tech company. We were fancy and clean except for the Coke bottle spittoon Donnie toted for his chaw dribblings. He wasn't shy about it like another boss I had who was more of a gentleman's dipper. Donnie would plant a monkey's fist in his cheek and chew away. Loud, Marlboro Country–smacking sounds followed by wet spits.

He was also incredibly abrasive, constantly berating me, his only direct report. It's rarely good when your power-loving boss only has one person to manage and it's you.

I used to get physically ill when I would pull into work and see his car. And if I didn't see it, I would imagine he was hiding it in an alley just to mess with me.

Donnie was my boss for about a year, and during that time I was miserable. I wanted to quit so badly I regularly daydreamed about announcing my two minutes' notice and bolting.

I longed to be free and away from him. I thought if I quit my job I wouldn't have to deal with such a horrible boss.

Wouldn't that be nice? Sayonara, Donnie. So long, control freak. So long, performance review.

In this land of no Donnies, we imagine waves of freedom and awesomeness washing over us. We assume that soon everything we ever wanted to do will be available. Not all at once perhaps—we are not that naïve—but at least we won't have to check with someone before we do something. At least we'll be in charge of all the decisions. We'll be the boss, not someone else!

The unfortunate truth is the land of no Donnies is just a fantasyland. The second you quit your bad boss you get dozens of new bosses. And some are more demanding than the Donnie you just left.

That can't be right. I quit. I left the land of micromanagement, the country of control freaks. I Bear Gryllsed right out of there. One can no longer draw a dotted line to me in an org chart. I am my own boss living off the corporate grid.

You are. But you aren't. You may have ditched Donnie, but you really just traded him in for a dozen mini Donnies.

Who are the new Dons in "You, Inc."?

The electric bill.

The water bill.

Chase Mortgage.

Pampers 120-packs.

Verizon Wireless.

Trader Joe's.

Johnny's Auto Repair.

Comcast Cable.

All the responsibilities that were quietly and almost magically covered when you had a steady job suddenly become your new and more demanding Dons. The wonderland of freedom feels more like wanderlust. Now you have a new set of worries. Now you've created dozens of tiny leaks in your lifeboat. And unless you're independently wealthy and you bought a case of this book simply as a kindness to the Acuff family, you'll spend far more time plugging those holes than steering your ship toward your dream.

Inanimate objects like bills are not the only new bosses you'll acquire. If you want to really stimulate your relationships with a spouse and family members, quit your job and make them your boss.

Few things are more romantic than a long, heated conversation with your wife about a ten-dollar book you purchased online instead of checking it out at the library. *It's only ten dollars,* you'll think, stupefied that you're having such conversations. *Are we really arguing about how long my showers are? We've been married for years; this might be our first water-bill debate.* But you'll have them. I promise you'll have them.

And when you're not fighting about money, which is suddenly an issue because you don't have any coming in, you'll reflect on how you spend your free time.

Don't be surprised when your previously supportive spouse casts an inquisitive eye on you as you unwind in front of the television. When you had your old job, that wasn't an issue. Watch some television at night or on the weekends. Go for it. Get that downtime you need, dear.

When that day job is gone, the lines between downtime and work time are blurred. It's all just time. And it's all heavy laden and economically laced. Downtime is suddenly time you could be spending improving your résumé or researching new prospects. Time you could be getting ahead or moving the ball forward. Time you should be spending not watching *Mad Men*, which is really just the thinking man's version of *Jersey Shore* anyway. Binge drinking? Check. Casual sex? Check. Northern accents? Check. Hopeless, hurt-inside stares? Check.

You think I am exaggerating, but quit your day job and see if your experience isn't eerily similar.

A friend of mine is going through this right now. He quit his day job. He's on his own and suddenly his wife wants to talk about how many cover letters and résumés he is sending out every day. Nothing, and I mean nothing, fires up your love life like a discussion with your spouse about whether you've met your cover letter quota. And I promise when he had a day job she never asked him how many reports he filed at work that day.

This is one of the largest quitting land mines we fail to see. When you chase your dream, you need the support of your partner. You need that person beside you every step of the way. That part of your life, the significant relationship quadrant as it were, needs to be rock solid and stable and in such a good place it's not clamoring about in crisis. Your dream job is loud and noisy and needs your focus, so your relationship needs to be in order to avoid the explosions. And even then you won't avoid them all.

Want to throw an easy relationship into chaos? Quit your day job.

The wife who never worried about money will have fiscal panic attacks. The husband who didn't tally how you spent your time will become an ever-present punch clock. Even the most easygoing person on the planet starts sweating when you play around with things like the mortgage. All in the name of your dream. Your dream? How do dreams pay the bills? Should you just dial up your utility providers and see if dreams are an acceptable form of payment? Is there a secret, free food section you have access to when you're married to a dreamer? As it turns out, no.

Family ties fare no better. It's bad enough they expect you to get married young and start popping out kids straightaway; now you'll get to discuss your income plans with your 70-year-old aunt over turkey and stuffing. Your well-read uncle will pass judgment with the mashed potatoes as he opines on the state of the economy.

This is a lose-lose-lose situation.

I want you to drop the q-bomb on Donnie. I do. Just not yet. And not under the belief that doing so will usher you into a gloriously bossless nirvana. There is a wiser way to get to your dream job, and it begins by keeping your day job.

Keep your no's open

Since I was a third grader at Doyon Elementary, a school that to this day makes me want to say "No Doy!" I dreamed about publishing a book. It was the only thing I consistently thought of whenever "dreams" came up. Over and over again this is what I returned to.

Having dreamt about a book deal for more than two decades, getting that first email from a publisher was an unbelievable feeling. This was it! This was the thing I had been working toward and sweating toward. It was all coming together, and I felt like rolling around in the book contract like Scrooge McDuck in his money bin.

I talked to the publisher for weeks. I had only been writing my blog for a few months, but they had picked up on what I was doing and were wildly interested. When your dream is something you started in your kitchen, it's easy to get wowed by someone real expressing interest in it. I was overwhelmed and sat in bed with my wife night after night talking it over.

But something was amiss. Something was wrong. Something didn't feel right.

We never want to see the worm in the apple we think is so shiny and delicious. Unfortunately, my publishing deal was indeed full of worms. Some friends who are authors confirmed how bad it was. Afraid of wrecking my dream, I went around and around on the numbers. There had to be something we could do. I held out hope, phone call after phone call, email after email. Finally, after weeks of conversations, the publisher said something to the effect of, "How about you let us publish the book without paying you anything for it? We'll sell it in stores, keep 100 percent of those profits for ourselves, and sell it back to you at a discounted rate so that you can sell it on your blog."

In that scenario, I would give them the book for free and then buy it back from them. That's like letting someone borrow your car and then paying him to let you drive it. It was a ridiculous offer.

But if I didn't have a job at that time, I'd have been in a really difficult position. When 100 percent of your future, 100 percent of your money, 100 percent of your dream is dependent on one thing succeeding, you are strongly tempted to compromise. You are tempted to cut corners. You are tempted to agree to less-than-perfect terms and sign less-than-perfect contracts. The risk of passing up any opportunity is extremely high.

But if you have a job—even a less-than-ideal one—you get to say a pretty vital word.

No.

I didn't have to agree to their terms. I didn't have to sign that horrible contract. Sitting safely in the comfort of my less-than-ideal day job, I passed. I said no and walked away.

You effectively lose that option when you quit. You lose that freedom when you jump without a net. You lose the power of the walkout or the shredded contract. Because

(handwritten in left margin: Marriage OR Work...)

you need this embarrassing gig. You need that horrible book deal. You need that lackluster partnership because the Dons are hungry and refuse to go away empty-handed.

On the other hand, when you still have your job you don't have to obsess about the consequences of saying no. You can instead focus on the benefits of saying yes to the right opportunities.

When you keep your day job, all opportunities become surplus propositions rather than deficit remedies. You only have to take the ones that suit your dream best.

Sure, you can still reject an opportunity on principle without a job. But there's a big difference in the consequences of principled rejection with a job and without one. Look no further than the births of my two daughters.

My daughter L.E. cost about a nickel. When my wife gave birth to her at Brigham & Women's in Boston, I threw a handful of sticky, cup holder coins at the receptionist, like a cheap version of Diddy.

My second daughter, McRae, cost about a million dollars. We were paying for our own health care because I didn't have a full-time day job. After seeing the bill for McRae's birth, I concluded she should have come out of the womb crying diamonds and clutching Benjamins in her baby fists.

Worse than this expectation was my thought-life before McRae was born. The doctors were fearful of an abnormality in her brain and wanted to run a lot of tests. In the middle of this horrific news, I thought to myself, *Wow, that's really expensive.*

Let me repeat that so you can fully grasp what a jerk I am.

My daughter needed a special ultrasound to properly assess a potentially serious medical condition. I worried about the cost.

Why?

Because the bill wasn't just my bill. It was my boss. The Don was demanding very high dues.

By the way, kids don't get cheaper when they're older either. My friend Matt quit his day job to pursue his dream job full time. When his elementary-aged daughter broke her arm, it cost his family $6,000 or a Kia to get her treated at the hospital.

So I'm grateful I found a way to close the gap between my day job and my dream. The Dons don't own me and I get to say no when I need to, especially when it comes to things like speaking.

THE FIVE CRITERIA I GO THROUGH WHEN I GET A NEW SPEAKING REQUEST:

1. Are they willing to pay my fee?

2. Will I be speaking to an influential crowd?

3. Will I be associated with other influential speakers at the event?

4. Will I already be in the area speaking somewhere else?

5. Is this a unique chance to share an important
   idea with a new audience?

When someone asks me to speak, there needs to be a yes to at least three of those questions before I say yes to the opportunity. Otherwise I say no. But guess what happens if I quit my day job and try to live out my dream job of speaking full time? My five-part criterion is reduced to one overwhelming question, "Are they willing to pay my fee?"

I lose the leverage to ask questions 2–5. I cash in that leverage when I quit my job. It doesn't matter if I disagree with one of the other conference speakers. It doesn't matter if the engagement is on the other side of the country and it will take me away from my wife and kids for days. It doesn't matter if I'll have to compromise my core message to fit the crowd's preferences.

I will say yes, or paying my bills will be hard that month. And my yes may not even be to my full fee. The Dons don't like discounts, but something is always better than nothing. Getting paid 50 percent of what I think I'm worth is a bruised shin compared to the broken nose of earning nothing that month. A desperate you and I will take that any day.

To chase your dream well you must fight to hold on to this small but significant word. Saying no is one of your most important resources, especially in the beginning. And the simplest and safest way to keep your no's is to keep your day job.

Stay dangerous

It is very possible you've actually thought long and hard about quitting your job. You're in the minority of folks who have saved up money for a famine year. The threat of a dozen new Dons doesn't worry you, at least not right away.

If you quit now, there is still another land mine looming you've probably not considered: remaining dangerous.

I learned about this threat when my first book came out. It turns out there were some people who did not like *Stuff Christians Like*.

This is understandable. It's a Christian satire of which there have been seven written since the invention of Gutenberg's printing press. The "Christian Satire" shelf does not exist at bookstores because it is not a category people aim for.

And despite being a Christian myself and never mocking faith, the book took some risks. The first line was, "If you buy this book, God will make you rich." The first chapter was about how we Christians sometimes rank honeymoon sex slightly higher than the second coming of Christ.

It was a little edgy, but family and friends were willing to laugh at this. My seventyish aunt told me she read the book from the back to the front as soon as she saw that first chapter. She apologized for not being able to give it to any of her Bible study friends. That kind of pushback was funny. When a radio station canceled my interview after receiving the book, it wasn't so funny.

They didn't like the content, and that made me nervous. Publishers don't like it when radio stations cancel on their authors. I didn't like hearing about bookstores trying to talk people out of buying it. One reader told me that when she brought it to the register the cashier said, "That book isn't edifying." Ouch.

The reason was that the content was dangerous. It was outside the norm of what is discussed within typical Christian circles. The book made people nervous even though it was by no means controversial. Why? Because dreams always make people nervous.

Dreams tend to challenge the status quo. They ask questions like, "Why do we do things this way?" and then assert, "Here is a better way." No one ever says, "I have an amazing dream that I am going to dedicate my life to. If it works, the status quo will be solidified forever!"

At the heart of a dream is change. Few like this. People get comfortable and often see dreamers as threats. We might be a culture that wants to quit our day jobs but deep down change still scares a lot of us, especially when it threatens the norms we've come to embrace. But if you're going to chase your dream job, guess what? You will be dangerous. You're going to threaten the status quo, and that's not for the faint-hearted.

There will be a long list of people who ask you to play it safe. At every corner, with every new opportunity will come a temptation to soften or dilute your dream. Other people will try to smooth out the edges for you. Outsiders will lob bricks. Decisions will force you to consider compromising your core idea and belief. Friends will tell you to change something, to remove part of whatever it is you're doing that's threatening because it's just not comfortable. Be careful, they'll say.

And if you don't have your day job, guess what? You will have to pacify them most of the time. You will have to choose the safer but less rewarding route.

Remember that list of new bosses you got when you quit your job? Your bills and your financial commitments and your spouse's expectations? Well, in addition to those Dons being demanding, they're also incredibly tight and inflexible. Even if you push them back with your savings and buy yourself a few months of risky but rewarding decisions, they will eventually show their stodgy side.

You might be surprised, but your monthly food budget isn't that open-minded. It's not great at embracing your vision.

Try as you might to explain the huge reward a particular risk offers, your electric bill isn't going to offer you creative deferment.

The only thing your new bosses will tell you over and over again is, "Be careful, be careful."

You'll start to worry about your future: "What if the people who pay for my dream don't like this idea? What if they're offended and cease being fans? Is this idea worth risking our savings account for? Is this idea worth sending our kids back to school in pants that don't fit?"

I was able to avoid a lot of these conversations by staying at my last day job years after I wanted to quit. I was able to skate past lots of temptations because I held on to that job. I was able to write for CNN because I had a day job.

They contacted me about writing for their website. If I didn't have a day job I might have considered the danger in talking to CNN and played it safe. As a Christian, I was well aware CNN was considered the devil's news. What if my Christian fans were super-conservative and hated my association with CNN? What if churches that booked me to speak found out and canceled my engagements? I tend to be pretty conservative and saw it simply as a great platform to share my ideas. But what if other people didn't see it that way?

The threat to my dream's momentum loomed large, until I remembered I still had a day job. Even if I lost every speaking gig I had booked for the next year, my wife and kids would be taken care of. My mortgage and food were not tied to my ability to sustain the status quo with a dream that was at its heart trying to break status quo.

Instead of compromising, I got to stay true to my dream. I got to write an honest, up-front article about why Christians like me can be jerks online. Hundreds of people didn't like it. Lots of people commented on it and said some pretty hateful things. But through it all, I got to stay dangerous. I got to stay focused on doing what I had set out to do.

I know it sounds crazy, but people with jobs tend to have more creative freedom than people without.

Want to stay dangerous with your dream? Want to make some real progress?

Don't quit your day job. Not yet.

The real reason you should stay put

My weight fluctuates from time to time by about twenty pounds. That last sentence made it sound like I don't have anything to do with it, like maybe the moon is the problem. It's not. It's me. Well, me and Gordo's.

Gordo's is a microwaveable queso dip that Walmart sells. I don't like sweets. I don't eat ice cream. But chips and queso kill me. That's easily my kryptonite. Still, I was okay for years when you couldn't make it gourmet at home.

After several failed attempts at boiling and heating my own cheese concoctions, I gave up and relegated myself to periodic bliss at Mexican restaurants. Then along came Gordo's. My life changed. My beltline followed suit.

I eventually looked down and shortly thereafter put myself on a slow carb diet that included no more Gordo's, which in Spanish means "fat," by the way.

I expected to lose weight and feel better physically, but something else happened that caught me off guard. As I dieted, I started to get more done at work. I started to write more on this book. I started to get up earlier and be more deliberate about spending time with my wife and kids. It wasn't instant. But over a period of weeks the momentum of more healthy eating spread to every part of my life. Why?

✻   Because discipline begets discipline.

When you step up to a challenge before you, your ramped-up resources rub off on other areas of your life. You wouldn't think eating less "fat" would impact how closely you monitor your family's financial budget, but it's all tied together. Discipline and focus are contagious and they tend to spread their benefits all around. Unfortunately this works both ways.

When you don't eat well or sleep enough or you get upside down on a car loan, it drags down the other parts of your life. This is particularly true when it comes to quitting your day job before you should. Especially for men.

Men need to work. I don't just mean that in a rustle-cattle-and-punch-mountain-lions-in-the-face kind of way. I'm a writer. I do not have calluses on my hands, and work-men who make repairs on my home address my wife, who has a degree in construction management. Wrenches puzzle me. I mean men need work in a purpose kind of way.

Men need a project and some progress at all times. (I think women need these things too, but having spent the last thirty-five years of my life on the boy side of the ball, this is the role I understand). I know men in their fifties who have not held full-time jobs for decades by their own decision. They're not injured or incapable of employment; they just don't like to be tied down and so they flitter about, "freelancing" now and then to make ends meet. Their marriages are falling apart. Coincidentally I've never met a wife who said, "Our marriage awakened the moment my husband quit working and stopped providing stability for the family."

A friend my age had the same situation. After a couple of years of working five-hour-a-week, part-time jobs, his life and marriage started to unravel. His wife was constantly burdened. She wanted to have kids but didn't see how that was possible with him contributing so little to the family's well-being. That makes sense to me. If I were a girl (a dangerous way to start a sentence), why would I expect you to be a committed, attentive, dedicated father if you couldn't dedicate yourself to something as simple as a day job? If humanity's chief needs include security and stability and you're not actively contributing to either, why would I trust you with another life, let alone my own?

This isn't an idea I invented. Thousands of people have written about the need and purpose of work in our lives. Actor Ryan Gosling dealt with this after the success of the movie *The Notebook*. To combat the sense of drifting aimlessly, he got a job making sandwiches at a deli. When asked about it in an interview he said, "The problem with Hollywood is that nobody works. They have meals. They go to Pilates. But it's not enough. So they do drugs. If everybody had a pile of rocks in their backyard and spent every day moving them from one side of the yard to the other, it would be a much happier place."[3]

We need to work.

And though I feel like I'm stepping on Oprah's toes here, if a guy or girl you're dating is lazy and jobless, chances are marriage is not going to jump-start things. Having a baby doesn't jump-start a marriage. Getting married doesn't jump-start a relationship. Quitting a job doesn't jump-start a dream because dreams take planning, purpose and progress to succeed. That stuff has to happen before you quit your day job. Often it should occur months and even years before. You've probably heard the axiom "Success always comes when preparation meets opportunity."[4] It's true, and the opportunity to quit your job will always be there. The real question is whether you've prepared.

Figuring it all out as you go is not a plan. Escaping imperfect circumstances is not a purpose. Quitting your job because it feels right is not progress. It's precisely the opposite.

Want to demonstrate love for your spouse or significant other? Keep your day job while you chase your dream job.

Want to learn how to be dedicated and focused on your dream? Practice being dedicated and focused at work.

Want to give your dream the best shot of success? Learn how to be successful at work.

We often demonize our day jobs when we dream. We make them enemies of what we really want to do. But if you dream the right way and learn how to quit the right way, your day job can actually be your dream job's greatest ally.

One last word about quitting your job, because maybe you should

Initially I was tempted to slam this chapter somewhere in the middle of the book.

My fear was that the casual reader, the girl at Urban Outfitters with a really complicated scarf, might be turned off by having the first chapter in a book about chasing your dreams begin with the assertion, "Don't quit your job." I understand that, I do.

It's common for dream-following books to start with encouraging chapters like, "Your dream is only one step away" or, "Dare to believe and it will all come true." And that's fine; there's a place for that I guess. I just didn't think that place was the beginning of this book.

Despite my extensive history of job quitting and the advice of scores of people, I didn't quit my day job at AutoTrader.com for three years. That probably doesn't seem like a long time to you but to me it is the equivalent of a twenty-one-year career. During this tenure, I started a blog that is read in 97 percent of the countries in the world, I wrote a book, I sold that book to more people than 95 percent of all authors do, I built two kindergartens in Vietnam, I was offered an additional two-book deal from one of the biggest publishers in the world, and I keynoted at conferences across the country.

Most of it would not have been possible without a day job that allowed me to duck the Dons, keep my no's, stay dangerous, and stabilize my marriage.

But eventually I did quit my day job for something else. Something crazy. And I think you might too. But before you do, we need to kill some popular but precarious lies about quitting.

CHAPTER 2

Removing The "I'm" From Your "But"

We love goodbyes.

I've never attended a "steadfast obedience" party at work. I've never been invited to a "staying put" get-together. I've never heard of a "sticking around forever" shindig. And I haven't for one simple reason: We live in a corporate culture that celebrates people who leave and ignores those who stay.

I don't blame them—there is something inherently sexy about quitting your job. You conjure up adventures and goatees and close calls in foreign lands with girls whose names have an attractive number of vowels. You can't help but think about the potential life someone will find out there in the wide world.

We get really drunk on the idea of what might be. We ignore what already is. We don't notice the person who comes in every day, tirelessly handling key components of a business week after week. We get starry-eyed about the adventure someone will inevitably have when he quits that same company. Think of the opportunities! Think of the dream! These are the things we exclaim at going-away parties held in our offices while eating mediocre grocery-store cake.

I remember the last time I attended a going-away party for a girl I knew. After nearly ten years of loyal service, she was quitting. In our city she was one of the highest paid in her field. She still had a lot of runway ahead of her. She was quitting anyway.

It was her last day and we were all there to talk about her. I wish I had a dollar for every time someone told her, "I'm so proud of you for following your dream and stepping out in courage." Over and over we lauded this girl with envy at her boldness, as if only cowards would stay at their jobs. We were so ashamed that we didn't have the guts to follow in her footsteps. Take these broken wings and learn to fly again, learn to live so free!

No one made a peep about doubting her decision. No one said the *i* word, *impulsive*. She was the emperor in brightly colored quitting clothes, and who were we to tell her otherwise? Worse still, she didn't even have another job or another plan to make money. She simply quit to follow a fuzzy feeling she had in her heart. We didn't care. She was our hero.

Labeling quitters automatic winners, coupled with the ready demonization of our jobs we talked about in Chapter 1, has had an interesting effect on us.

It has turned us into the "I'm, but" Generation.

We don't know what we want, but this isn't it

When I speak to people online or in person, we inevitably end up talking about what they do. Hundreds, if not thousands of times, I find one thread of consistency in the explanations I hear.

People say:

"*I'm* a teacher, *but* I want to be an artist."

"*I'm* an accountant, *but* I want to be a therapist."

"*I'm* a project manager, *but* I want to start my own company."

At first I was surprised by this because I think the perception is that if you're unhappy at work, you must not know what you want to do. If you're not in love with your current job, you must not know how to finish the "I'm a _____, but I want to be a _____" assertion. But that wasn't what I found to be true.

If anything, most of us have at least a blurry definition of what we'd like to do if we could. No one ever told me, "I'm a pharmacist, but I have no idea what I want to be. Absolutely zero idea really. Never had a dream, never had a desire, never had something that made me feel alive. I am a blank canvas of misery in the pharmacy where I work." No, there was always at least a hint of some other desire, dream or expectation for life.

I don't think we're confused about what we want to be when we grow up. We might not be able to say, "I want to become a CPA and open my own business on 10th Street in Cleveland, Ohio, in March of 2014," but for the most part we've had a glimpse of our dream job.

And even if we don't know precisely what our thing is or our passion, there are plenty of ways to find out.

For instance, according to the Myers-Briggs Personality Assessment, I am an "ENFP."

That means I am into extroversion, intuition, feeling and perception. According to that personality test, those four letters indicate a lot about me. I'm friendly, I'm a global thinker, I like people, etc. My favorite part of the analysis, though, is the list of people who are also ENFPers. One site lists Sinbad and Bill Cosby as fellow ENFPers. Their one distinguishing credit for Cosby is that he was in *Ghost Dad*. Why didn't they mention that slightly popular series called *The Cosby Show*? Would you ever in your life describe Bill Cosby as "that guy who was in that movie *Ghost Dad*?" The best part of this web analysis is it also lists fictional ENFPers. Want to know who I am like? Balkie from *Perfect Strangers*, Ariel from *The Little Mermaid* and Urkel from *Family Matters*.

Awesome. That is quite a motley crew.

According to the DISC profile's rankings of 0–100, I scored 100 points on I and 0 points on C. *I* stands for Influence and *C* stands for Conscientiousness. So I'll be able to convince you to do something, but you'll probably think I'm a jerk during the experience. I am also wildly different in my natural life (who I really am) and my adapted life (who I am in public). There is actually a 60-point gap between those two ratings, and considering it's a 100-point scale, that is troubling.

According to another test, I am an ideation guy. A different one rated me as an "otter." A Christian test said that I am a "Jacob."

There is no shortage of personality tests and job tests out on the market. And I have taken a lot of them. Some are great and deeply inform you about some questions you might have about your life. Some feel a little fluffy, like a fortune-teller who asks broad questions and gives you even broader answers.

That is why I am a little hesitant to put a chapter in here about figuring out what your dream is. It would be easier if we all just knew. It would be easier if we came onto the planet with that written out clearly. That is not the case.

If it were, I would not have been a horrible guitar player for about thirty minutes.

That's how long I was willing to dedicate to the craft. I owned a Martin D1, which is an expensive, beautiful guitar. Upon which I was able to play the opening to "Every Rose Has Its Thorn," by the band Poison. Perhaps you are familiar with this exquisite ballad.

I was also a horrible painter for about thirty minutes.

I thought that maybe what I wanted to do was paint. So I took an accomplished local painter to an art store. She encouraged me to spend $200 on really fancy paints. Then I went home, sat in the yard, and painted a still life. Of a Diet Coke can. Then I quit.

I was a horrible runner for about 2 hours and 39 minutes.

That's how long it took me to run a half marathon. I thought maybe I could be a runner. Shave my legs, get all skinny, and own yellow sneakers. (Only really fast or crazy people are allowed to own yellow running shoes.) I was going to do it this time. For real. I was going to be a runner. But after my first race, I spent an hour in the bathtub, finally being forced out by my wife, who was leaving to run errands and was concerned I would drown.

I'm not a guitar player.

I'm not a painter.

I'm not a runner.

I'm a writer, something it took me decades to remember. Decades I don't want you to waste. Decades I want you to enjoy doing what it is you want to do with your life.

I'd much rather us figure it out, capture it, even, and get you started today than have you spin your wheels like me for many years.

So what do you want to do?

I have exactly one idea about that question, but I think it is surprisingly enough.

The 42-year-old new beekeeper

Whenever you start trying to actively figure out what it is you want to do, whenever you start to search for the thing that makes you come alive, something weird happens. You imagine you are going to discover it.

You might not verbalize this, but inside you start to think that when you finally land upon what it is you are supposed to be doing with your life, it will be a pleasant surprise. We all tend to view the process of finding our dream job like arriving at our surprise birthday party. We imagine we will take a personality test, arrive at the results and be blown away. Like we never saw it coming.

"Circus acrobat? Wow! And I'm an accountant. No wonder these years have been so hard. I should be in the circus."

We think finding out what we want to do is going to be a revelation. In our twenties or thirties or forties, **we will** serendipitously stumble upon some activity we've never done and like a kid tasting ice cream for the first time, we'll be hooked. Lightbulb! Turns out we like beekeeping. Although we've always appreciated honey as a concept and definitely in Cheerios, we've never had a fascination with queen bees and hives. But suddenly we want to spend time around bees. A lot of time in a lot of weird suits with smoke and local farmers who have braids in their beards.

That's what we believe about our dreams. But dreams rarely work that way.

In his book *Start with Why*, author Simon Sinek discusses this reality. He calls our dreams, or calling, our "WHY." He says, "The WHY for every individual or organization comes from the past. It is born out of the upbringing and life experience of an individual."[5] He further explains that finding WHY is not a process of "invention." I agree with that. And I would take it one step further.

I think finding your dream job or what Sinek calls your WHY is more than a revelation or an act of discovery. I believe it's a process of recovery.

More often than not, finding out what you love doing most is about recovering an old love or an inescapable truth that has been silenced for years, even decades. When you come to your dream job, your thing, it is rarely a first encounter. It's usually a reunion. So instead of setting out to discover this thing you love doing, you've got to change your thinking and set out to recover it, maybe even rescue it.

Why?

Because somehow you lost it along the way. I think this happens for a few reasons.

For one thing, you might not have been ready for it the first time around. I once heard Bono tell Bill Hybels in an interview that in the 80s, he and his wife visited Ethiopia and saw the tremendous need there first-hand. On the way home, he told his wife, Ali, "We will never forget this." She responded, "You know we will because to carry this with you everyday is too much." Bono reflected on that moment and said despite that, "We were both clear that at some point, we would be called upon to revisit these questions that in truth were probably too big for our young minds."[6]

The young, rising star was not ready to start his work with One, the charity organization, in 1985. He was not yet a philanthropist interacting with people like Desmond Tutu and Nelson Mandela. He was an up-and-coming musician who needed to grow before he could actually step into his calling. Still, it was there. And in the 90s he and his calling were reunited for good.

Your dream might not be as extreme as Bono's, but like him you may meet yours before you're ready to run after it. That's what happened to me with blogging. In 2001, before it was a verb, my friend Billy and I started a website that specialized in music interviews, book reviews and pop culture. I ran it for a year and could have gotten in on the ground floor of that medium, but I wasn't ready to handle the commitment. It would be seven years later and multiple blogs before I would start Stuff Christians Like. By that time, I was better prepared. When 4,000 people showed up on day eight of its existence, I was able to handle an influx that would have wrecked me in 2001.

Another thing that estranges us from our dreams is everyday distraction. Rarely is the distraction so large you notice it. I've never met someone who says, "I was unable to write my great American novel because my house burned down." Instead, I've met hundreds of people who tell me they've never written their books because they are too busy. When you are in college, it's easy to daydream what you'll be when you grow up. You have huge chunks of time for the pursuit of whatever. But the chunks turn to crumbs when you hit the real world.

There are bills and babies and jobs. You've got a calendar that barks out marching orders and multiple email accounts to manicure each day. When life gets full, it's a shame that your dream is one of the first things to get lost in the fray. We stop painting in our spare time or designing on the weekends because it seems such a fruitless endeavor. What a silly way to spend our free time when we could be getting that much-deserved rest or that much-needed mall therapy. You and your dream lose touch and then years or decades later, like that summer-camp love September stole away, we bump back into our dreams and that bittersweet beckoning. "Ohhh, I remember you."

Even then, some of us don't want to acknowledge the former feelings. We play dumb. This comes out in my own life when I try to write. The hardest part of writing for me is being honest. It's not that I want to lie—I don't set out that way, but if I'm not careful I end up playing the role of a clever writer instead of writing something that is true of my own experience and helpful to others.

My wife pointed this out when I wrote my first book. She read an early chapter, paused and then confessed, "I think it's well-written, it's just that the whole thing is a lie."

That's not fun feedback to get at the kitchen table. But she was right. I wasn't writing the book I wanted to write. I was writing the book I thought I should write. I was sitting down and trying to copy the writing of other authors. I was writing Donald Miller's book or Tim Ferriss' book.

Why?

Because I had discounted my dream. I was afraid to give credence to those often frightening feelings that come with wanting something fervently.

In a contrarian version of "the grass is always greener," we tend to discount the value, importance and urgency of our own dreams. In a subtle form of self-preservation, we find ourselves rejecting compliments people give us for doing what we love. When someone notices we're good at something, we respond:

"Oh that, that's nothing. It's just something I like to do in my spare time."

The soundtrack we play in our minds is that our gift is nothing. Our dream really isn't that meaningful. It is just a bit of gossamer we play with sometimes. Don't think twice about it.

The longer you play this soundtrack, the easier it is to believe it, especially if someone who matters to you tells you that your dream doesn't matter. Teachers, bosses, sometimes even parents will tell you that you're not good enough to pursue a particular dream. The more we develop the muscle of doubt, the stronger it becomes. But the doubt is still a deception.

If you recognize that, if you admit that there is a chance that you are good, perhaps even great at something, you should feel a little uncomfortable. Because if your gift is not nothing, that means it is something. And a gift that is something is always a little terrifying, for at least three reasons:

1. **Nothing can't hurt you.**
   If your gift is something, then the pull to explore it is always there. You are compelled even if only by curiosity to at least try. Maybe you won't jump off a cliff for this something, but your chances of getting hurt are dramatically greater from pursuing something than nudging up to nothing.

2. **Nothing is comfortable.**
   Call it the "better the devil you know than the devil you don't know" syndrome. We're familiar with the nothing lie. It feels like an old sweater at this point, and we like that. The unknowns of a dream are just too disconcerting. What evils might arise? We'd rather not find out.

3. **Nothing is normal.**
   People with somethings are weird. In his book *Orbiting the Giant Hairball: A Corporate Fool's Guide to Surviving with Grace*, Gordon MacKenzie says that if you ask a roomful of first graders, "How many artists are there in the room?" they all eagerly raise their hands. If you ask a roomful of third graders, only a third of the class raises their hands. MacKenzie laments, "The higher the grade, the fewer children raised their hands. By the time I reached sixth grade, no more than one or

two did so and then only ever-so-slightly—guardedly—their eyes glancing from side to side uneasily, betraying a fear of being identified by the group as a closet artist."[7] And it's not just art that we feel that way about. It's dreams too. We are embarrassed to have big, unruly somethings and would much rather go with the flow and have a normal life like everyone else. Not at thirty or even twenty years old. We begin thinking this way at eleven or twelve.

***

So what do you do when you find yourself buying the nothing lie? You read this chapter and everything will be magically fixed.

I wish that were the case, but you usually can't just eject a soundtrack of doubt or denial that's been playing for years.

What you can do—and it's really the best place to start—is call the soundtrack what it really is. A lie. You might still hear it. You might put this book down and hear it louder than you ever have before. But a lie is still a lie. And a lie is no foundation on which to base your career decisions.

Don't buy into the nothing lie. You wound yourself when someone compliments your gift and you reply, "Oh, that's nothing." Your gift is never nothing. Regardless of what it can be, it is always something. And something is the perfect place to start.

There is a deep, deep hope seated in the idea that finding a dream is an act of recovery. There is a huge worth-the-price-of-this-entire-book difference between trying to discover your something and trying to recover your something.

When you ask the question, "What do I want to do with my life?" you should feel at least a little overwhelmed. There are a million possible answers to that question. Where do you begin? A sport I'm pretty good at? A hobby? A city where I'd like to live? Should I take a cooking class or a tango class? Should I go back to school and get a degree or just grow a really great garden? Of all the countless paths I could take, which one leads me home?

It's exhausting. The question, "What do I want to do with my life?" is nearly impossible to answer confidently and concisely, and that's because it's a discovery question. You're really asking, "How do I discover what I want to do with my life?" That is a question that points you into the vast expanse of the entire universe for an answer. It might sound fun, but once you're there it can quickly swallow you up.

But if finding your dream is an act of recovery, that changes everything.

You don't ask the bottomless, "What do I want to do with my life?" but instead, "What have I done in my life that I loved doing?" Instead of a million different options from out there, you're suddenly left with a manageable handful of options from within your own experience. Instead of trying to hitch your star to an endless black hole of options, you hitch a ride on your rewarding past.

Once you make this mental switch, you can immediately start combing through your history for hints that will reveal your something. My favorite way to do this is by looking for hinge moments.

In search of the hinge

Mercedes-Benz had a problem. They had developed an incredibly expensive sports car. It was an SLR and it cost more than $400,000, or as I like to think of it, "Double my first house." Although the production run of this particular beast was fairly limited, they still wanted to make sure each one sold.

In order to do that, every inch of the car needed to scream high-end performance. Every detail had to be perfectly matched to the power and luxury the car offered drivers. The engine had to be extraordinary. The doors needed to be gateways to an adventure, not just a matter of ingress into a car. The ignition had to be igniting.

When you think about it, the way we start our cars has not changed all that dramatically over the years. Once we moved beyond the arm-breaking cranks that were on the grilles of Model Ts, little progress happened to the actual ignition.

Miles per gallon, aerodynamics, heated seats and automatic doors—almost every part of the car has gone through a revolution of design improvement, except for the ignition. It has essentially remained the same for decades. You put a key in. You turn it. The car turns on. You drive.

But if the car in question is the Mercedes-Benz SLR, a standard ignition will not suffice. You can't go ordinary in an extraordinary vehicle.

So Mercedes looked at some improvements that have been made in the last twenty years. Some drivers seemed to really enjoy push-button ignitions. There's something inherently fun about pushing a button to start your car. But it's also fairly common at this point. You can get a push-button ignition in a Toyota Camry or a Honda Accord. It's not that special anymore.

The first thing Mercedes did is relocate the ignition button. While other manufacturers tend to place it in the dashboard, Mercedes put it in the gearstick. Right away, that feels a little different. Now starting your car feels a little like turning on a video game. That's interesting and a good start, but this is a $400,000 car. We have to move way beyond interesting.

What Mercedes-Benz did next forever changed the way I look at my life. That is a big statement, but I assure you it is not an exaggeration. It literally rewired how I look at what it means to follow a dream and do the things you love in life. It turned my understanding of what it takes to recover what you want to do upside down.

What did Mercedes-Benz do to the ignition button?

They added a hinge.

On top of the button they put a small hinge that held a cover in place. In order to start the car, you had to first open the cover and then press down on the ignition button with your thumb.

That simple hinge tapped into every scene in every movie where someone launches a missile. *The Hunt for Red October, Crimson Tide, Top Gun*—in any scene where the hero is about to launch an attack to vanquish a seemingly impossible foe, he must first open the cover and engage the hinge.

Suddenly, with a simple hinge, Mercedes-Benz forever altered the experience of its car. When you got into the SLR, you weren't starting a car, you were launching a missile out of your garage. With an incredibly simple hinge, Mercedes imbued their vehicle with an undeniable amount of emotion and energy.

I knew they understood what they had done when I saw their brochure for the SLR. It was only a few pages long, so they were only able to put photos and information about the most critical elements in it. On one page was a photo and explanation of the engine. It probably took years and millions of dollars to develop. On the other page? Mercedes put a close-up of the hinge.

It probably cost $30. It might have only taken them a few days to come to the conclusion to add it to the car. It was incredibly small and insignificant when taken out of context. But none of that mattered. None of that made a difference, because the hinge was the most important part of that vehicle.

Sometimes we think we need a massive eureka moment to come to grips with who we want to be and what we want to do. We wait for the lightning strike that will completely redefine our lives and give us clear direction.

But the truth is, the greatest impact tends to come from hinge moments.

A hinge moment occurs when you are planning to do something standard and normal, something you've done many times before, like turn a key in the ignition. And then seemingly out of nowhere, something, a small detail usually, hinges you in a different direction. A chance encounter at the grocery store, a stranger's random comment, one line in an article you read pushes you to a place you were not expecting to go. Two such occurrences come to mind from my own life.

Mrs. Harris and my first book

When people ask me when I knew I wanted to be a writer, this is the moment to which I most consistently point back. While living in Ipswich, Massachusetts, my third-grade teacher, Mrs. Harris, challenged me to write a book. I'm not sure why since the class was not writing books at the time. But regardless of the reason, she tasked me with writing a book and that's exactly what I did. After school each afternoon, I wrote poetry on those brownish sheets of paper with the red and blue lines and mile-wide margins.

The poems weren't great. I remember rhyming "fall" and "tall" an awful lot. We didn't sell any copies. I didn't walk away with a lightning-strike moment in those cold New England afternoons spent dulling my pencil. But it felt true. Even at that age, it felt like something I really liked doing and something I just assumed everyone else liked to do. (There's a natural feeling to the things we're called to that we often assume everyone else has.) Nothing dramatic happened with that book, except Mrs. Harris did a few things with it.

She laminated it.

She bound it.

She made me feel like I was a published author.

That was monumental for me. She didn't tell me I was an author. Those words never left her mouth. She didn't write that on a note in the book. She simply put the book together and handed it to me.

Suddenly, I was an author. The lamination sealed it, literally and metaphorically. It meant the world to me and though I couldn't tell you about anything I wrote for the next five years, that was a flare sent high up in the sky of my childhood. That was the very first hinge moment I can remember where I thought writing might be something I could do forever.

My dad gets the mail

My dad never got the mail when I was a kid. Well, almost never, because as a pastor who was trying to raise boys carefully, he had some sort of sixth sense when it came to the *Sports Illustrated* Swimsuit Issue. He could go a full 11 months and 29 days without getting the mail, but then on

Swimsuit Issue day, he flashed on the scene like a phantom, grabbed the thing, and threw it in the trash before my brothers and I knew what had happened. That was one of the two times he got the mail.

The other was my second hinge moment.

We didn't talk about it at the time. We haven't talked about it in the last twenty years. But when I was a teenager, he did something that spoke again to that third grader who liked to write about trees.

One night, he grabbed the mail and found me downstairs. He handed me a thick packet with a brown envelope attached. Unbeknownst to me, he'd sent away for a special kit on how to publish a book. I don't know if he paid for it or if it was just one of those things you could get for free because they wanted to sell you something. It didn't matter.

Here was a thick, "You are important to me, you could be a writer if you wanted to be" packet. I think he might have spoken three or four sentences about it and then we never discussed it again. I opened it and was excited but ultimately never followed through on it. I was a girl-obsessed, awkward teenage boy and writing a book seemed difficult and time consuming.

But that moment was part of the fuel that made me feel like my first book was in fact possible. That moment was forever etched in my memory as something that supported my belief that I could actually do this thing called writing. My dad believed in me. My dad believed in me so much that he had a packet for professional writers sent to me!

That was my second hinge moment. And I can still speak about it like it happened yesterday.

A few questions to ask when interviewing hinge moments

Looking back on it, the Mrs. Harris poetry book in the third grade was a bit like a Hallmark Movie of the Week. There I was, living on the North Shore of Massachusetts in a town that literally had a castle on the coast. My father was in seminary and painting houses to make ends meet. We didn't have a lot, but I did have my poetry and that kept me warm on those New England winter nights when the dark seemed hungry and the snow merciless.

That's a bit much, but the truth is that hinge was not difficult to spot. Looking back on it, the idea that a teacher would tell you she thought you were talented and actually use her free time to put together your first book is a stand-out moment. But not all hinges are that neon.

Most of the time I think they're a bit harder to recover. They're buried sometimes and you have to unearth them.

I thought just now about suggesting an egg-drawing technique I once learned about, but the more I wrote about it the more I felt like you should be lying down on a couch and I should have a counselor's beard, simply saying, "Hmmm, yes, please go on." So instead of asking you to color with crayons or unpack your issues, I think we can identify some of your hinge moments by knowing the right questions to ask.

**QUESTIONS I FOUND HELPFUL WHEN FIGURING OUT
MY OWN HINGE MOMENTS:**

1. **What do I love enough to do for free?**
   That's a cliché you sometimes hear in guidance coun-
   selors' offices in high school, but it's no less true. What
   would you do even if no one paid you for it? I blogged
   for about two years and didn't make a dime. I didn't
   need to. I wasn't writing for money. I was writing because I am a writer and that's what writers do.

2. **What do I do that causes time to feel different?**
   When you really get engaged in your something, space
   and time seem to shift a little. You'll sit down to do a
   little writing before dinner and the next time you look
   up it's ten and you never ate. Time shifts when you're
   doing what you love. Has that ever happened, and if so,
   what were you doing?

3. **What do I enjoy doing regardless of the opinions of
   other people?**
   Your dream can't be powered by opinion or affirmation. It has to be bigger than the feedback of a peer or a
   coworker. What would you do even if no one ever told
   you they loved it?

4. **If only your life changed, would that be enough?**
   If you killed yourself for years creating something
   and at the end of the experience, the only life that
   had changed was your own, would that be rewarding

enough? If the experience was the lesson and the journey itself was the reward, would that be okay with you? Is there something that holds that sway for you?

5.   **Are there any patterns in the things you like doing?**
     If you've got a dream, chances are there's not just one isolated hinge moment in your past. More than likely, you have a list of moments that are similar and related. What patterns can you see in the decisions you've made and the experiences you've loved?

Ask yourself those questions. Love yourself enough to actually write down your answers. And when you do, show them to someone you trust. Sometimes we're so close to the painting we can't tell what it is and we need someone else to point out the truth.

There is a word of caution about the two hinge moments I gave as examples. Those were both happy examples, times when someone reinforced what felt like a dream I had inside of me or when someone complimented a natural talent I thought I possessed. But don't confuse a hinge moment with a happy moment. Some of my most pivotal hinge moments were not particularly happy events. They were discouraging moments that didn't create a rainbow path for me to follow but instead clarified that a particular path was by no means going to work out for me. Like that afternoon I spent in a real advertising agency.

I didn't cry when I got back in the car with my mother-in-law, but it was only because I didn't want to miss my flight. Plus, when flying out of Atlanta, it's always best to save your tears for the airport. It will break you. It's a mash-up of Mad Max's thunderdome and overbooked flights that run on "ish" time. As in, "You'll fly out at four-ish" or, "Your plane isn't here yet but should be soon-ish."

But that day I had another reason to get teary. Prior to getting in the car with my mother-in-law, I had spent two hours inside an advertising agency trying to get a job. My wife and I lived outside of Boston in Arlington, Massachusetts, but we wanted to move to Georgia. We'd had our first daughter, the snow was killing my Floridian wife, and it was time to move closer to family.

But I couldn't find a job.

On my first flight down to have breakfast with a friend's contact, the person I met with refused to accept a copy of my résumé. The entire purpose of the trip was to meet this person and in our unexpectedly terse breakfast meeting he said, "I don't know anyone in Atlanta in advertising and no, I don't want a copy of your résumé."

That meeting was not particularly awesome, but he actually did know someone in Atlanta in advertising. His relative worked at an ad agency and over a period of weeks I arranged a meeting with her.

I spent days and days putting together my portfolio, a copywriter's toolkit to showcase the best work they've done. At the time I thought working at an ad agency was my dream. I was really proud of the work I had already accomplished at a small advertising agency and in the marketing departments of corporations I had worked for.

I showed up bright and early at the meeting, in a shirt from the "look fancy" part of my closet. This wasn't an interview though. Nobody in Atlanta would see me for an interview. I spent that day driving around Atlanta with my mother-in-law, who lived there, dropping off résumés and mini portfolios at any agency I could find. I researched the names of a dozen creative directors in the city. Then I would walk into advertising agencies and ask the receptionist to "please give this to Bill Smith."

So although I had flown down for the sole purpose of meeting this contact at an ad agency, this was not something formal or promising. I was desperate at this point and greatly appreciated the twenty casual minutes she gave me talking about what it was like to work in advertising in Atlanta.

On the way out she walked me by someone's office and said, "You should meet Mark." Turns out Mark was an Atlanta advertising expert. In addition to working at the biggest agencies in town, he taught at the The Creative Circus, a two-year advertising master's program. Mark invited me into his office and we ended up talking for an hour. He asked to see my portfolio, the one I had killed myself to put together. I thought, *Here comes my big break!*

By page two, he was shaking his head in disappointment. I don't remember if he even finished looking at the entire thing because my head started to spin and I thought I was going to throw up. What I do remember is that he took out two other portfolios. A good one and a bad one. He showed me what a copywriter's portfolio should look like and it was nothing like mine. I wasn't even close to his bad example. Six years into my career and my portfolio was pitiful.

At that point I just wanted to roll out a smoke bomb, slide to the floor and crawl for the parking lot where my mother-in-law was waiting patiently. But the experience wasn't over. Mark called the admin in and asked for the box of portfolios from people who had submitted them to this agency in hopes of getting a job. It was the size of a coffin for a pony. He then said, "Sit at an empty desk and go through these. See what you can learn."

In the middle of an office I'd never been in, without cubicle walls, I sat at someone's seat who was out to lunch and started leafing through dozens of portfolios from people who were better than me. It was meant as a lesson, and Mark was incredibly kind to me that day, but it was an immensely discouraging experience.

Looking back on it now, I can see how hinge moments like that and a few others changed my focus from advertising. I didn't want to be in advertising. I didn't want to be one more portfolio kept in one more box in the dust under one more assistant's desk. Removing advertising from my dream, coming up against that hard wall, subtracting that option from the list of things I was dreaming about, helped me focus on what I really loved.

I didn't love advertising. I got all the wrong answers when I asked advertising my hinge moment questions. I loved insight and writing. Advertising was just an execution of insight. The core of what I loved to do was insight. And that hinge moment, though painful and shared with my mother-in-law, swung me closer to pursuing what I loved.

For some of us, recognizing the hinge moments isn't the most difficult part. We've dreamed about our something for years. We're familiar with the 30,000-foot view. It's seeing things at 10,000 feet and then ten feet and then from the ground that's so difficult. That's when the obstacles really show up. Anyone can dream; it's the doing that is such a hassle.

CHAPTER 3

What Lies Between a Day Job and a Dream Job

You didn't have to be Scooby-Doo to figure out something was wrong with the house we were trying to buy in Tennessee. The property disclosure agreement, a legally binding document, indicated that there were zero repairs made to the house in the entire time the owner lived there. We wanted to believe that, we did. We thought the house was charming. The neighborhood was adorable. When it was Halloween, they had a big block party. At Christmas, a decorating contest with official prizes. When it snowed, they held a snowman contest. Bluebirds would land on your shoulder when you walked to the mailbox and sing you a jaunty tune. But something was decidedly wrong with the house.

How did we come to this conclusion?

The owner had written notes in Sharpie on the attic rafters, indicating to repairmen where all the roof leaks were. Ah, but maybe we're just being fancy—it's just the roof. Fair enough. But then we got in the crawl space and found buckets collecting water. How could they have possibly left buckets to collect water and at the same time told us the house was in perfect shape? But, who doesn't like water, right? It's life-giving. It's awesome. Maybe we could overlook that. We tried to, I promise, but the final straw, or rather the final ninety-eight-strawed straw, was the ninety-eight-point home inspection list we received.

If you've never bought a house, those weren't ninety-eight compliments the home inspector made. Those were ninety-eight things that needed fixing, ranging from "minor repair" to "this house will steal your soul."

The smart thing to do would have been to walk—no run—away from this particular house. My father-in-law is a homebuilder. My mother-in-law is a homebuilder. My wife has her master's in construction management and used to be a real estate agent. We are not dumb when it comes to homes; and when I say "we" I mean "they." But we still had a hard time walking away from what appeared to be a money pit. The reason is that we were getting slammed by one of the costs of chasing our dream—risk.

Every dream has risk associated with it. Some might have more than others, but each dream comes wrapped in some degree of risk. If it doesn't, it's not really a dream.

The one risk we were facing in this exact moment surrounded our finances. By accepting my dream job and joining the Dave Ramsey team, my salary had decreased. Over time there was a great potential to make great money, but for the first year or so things were going to be in a bit of flux. For the first six months, I'd have a steady base salary, but after that, the salary would decrease and our life would be funded in part by the commissions I made.

We didn't love that leaky-roofed house, but we were afraid that if we waited too long to buy one, we wouldn't be able to get a good loan. It was easier to secure a loan when I had the first six months of salary to show versus the flip-flop, inconsistent world of commissions. I might believe that I'd make dramatically more in the second six months of my first year, but the bank wouldn't believe that. So we started to panic and thought, *We better lock in this loan and buy this house while we can because if we wait we'll never get a good loan.*

The entire logic of that fear is messed up, but fear is rarely logical. Locking in a loan we might not be able to afford would have been an incredibly stupid thing to do and against everything the company I work for believes. Buying a house with a faulty roof, water in the crawl space and ninety-eight other problems would have been a foolish thing to do. But when the risks of chasing a dream show up and we allow fear to ride in on their coattails, we often make some really horrible decisions. And it all starts with how we decide to look at risk.

The magnifying glass, the kaleidoscope and the telescope

Risks are coming. In the next chapter we'll talk about some significant ways to mitigate them, but it doesn't make sense to pretend you won't face any. You will. How you perceive them will largely determine how successful you are at overcoming them.

In general, there are three different ways we look at the risks associated with a dream.

1. The Magnifying Glass

Sometimes when we're afraid of a risk, we look at it through a magnifying glass. We stare intently at it, blowing the possible consequences way out of proportion. We stare so closely at the risk that it fills our entire field of vision. We lose all sight of the possible reward a dream offers. We allow the risk to dominate the dream and define the future. If we've failed in the past, we start magnifying that experience too. We do not say, "I failed." We say, "I am a failure." Friends and family members will try to show us all the things we've lost sight of but we will not hear it. They don't have the same magnifying glass we do.

2. The Kaleidoscope

The best definition of creativity I ever heard from someone was that it is "a wild mind with a disciplined eye." A highly creative person has the ability to feed his mind all these different topics and ideas, then see a connection between previously unconnected things in a way no one has ever seen before. That definition is what makes the kaleidoscope view of risk so difficult for creative people. With this perspective, you look at your risk as if you're peering through a kaleidoscope tube. Instead of brightly colored jewels or mirrors that scramble the image you see, you add in parts of your life. The risk of your dream is no longer a risk that impacts one or two areas of your life—your career and your finances. It is now connected to every other aspect of your life. For instance, in our house situation, when I looked through the kaleidoscope, here is what I saw:

"This house looks like it has a lot of issues, but if we don't buy it, we'll never be able to get a loan. And if we can't get a loan, we'll have to rent somewhere else. L.E. will eventually have to go to her fourth school in four years. Our kids won't be able to walk to school. They'll probably hate a different school and get picked on. They'll be so sad we left Atlanta. The stress of constantly getting rejected from loan offers will probably be a lot of strain on my wife. And in order to find a place we can rent, we'll have to move thirty minutes away from her community of friends. We'll never be able to replace those friends and will probably end up homeless and friendless and I'll have to grow a patchy beard because I can't afford razors. The end."

It's ridiculous, I know. But if you've ever looked through a kaleidoscope, you know that what you see is never what's really there. The same thing happens when you look at risk in this way. Your fears and your worries are jumbled and multiplied a thousand times over until you lose sight of what is really before you.

3. The Telescope

When my daughters were young, they used to be horrible at hide-and-seek. Like most kids, they believed if they couldn't see you, you couldn't see them. So instead of hiding they would just close their eyes and stand completely still. We often do the same thing with risk. But it's still there. And if we ignore it, we can't plan for it, prepare for it or protect ourselves from it. That's why the telescope method is my favorite approach.

Telescopes are designed to view things that are far away, and that's where most of our risks are too. They haven't happened yet, they're in the future, and they live in the land of "What if?" When you look at a risk through a telescope, you're able to create a safe distance between your dream and your fears. You can see the risk in detail, but you acknowledge that a lot can happen in the space between you and that risk becoming reality.

You acknowledge it's there, you see it, but you're not allowing it to dominate your decisions. It's just one possible outcome. And by seeing it a long way out, you can make plans to reduce your chances of arriving at that outcome.

We'll talk more about a specific way to create a telescope with a risk list in Chapter 8, but before we get there we need to identify some of the common but unnecessary risks that trip us up, because risk is what's ultimately holding you back from pursuing your dream. We're going to clear them out of the way so you can start closing the gap between your day job and your dream job.

The problem with perfection

When things were out of control in my room on Edgewood Drive in Hudson, Massachusetts, my mom would ask me to clean up. I didn't tidy or make my bed. I didn't put the obvious piles of dirty laundry in the right room or clean off my desk. I always tried to go from a messy room to operating-room cleanliness in one afternoon. I didn't merely pick up books off the floor; I dusted the shelf slowly and re-arranged them by size or author name or both. I spent hours and hours on a two-foot square in my room, wanting everything to be perfect. About midway through, I would get overwhelmed at the task and give up.

My mom called me a "procrastinating perfectionist." I would wait until the last minute and then try to do it all perfectly and at once.

And maybe you think that way too.

The goal of this book is to get you to do what you love, with the life you already have. But there's a chance you feel like you've missed some of your opportunity. Whether you're seventeen or forty-seven, there's always the temptation to think that something has "passed us by." And now that we feel a little buzz to get things going, now that we feel a little momentum starting to build, it's easy to get a touch of procrastinating perfectionism. And that tends to cripple our ability to finish.

I want us to be a generation of finishers. I want us to be a generation of people who follow through and sew the last stitch or give the final keynote or write the last chapter.

And in order to get there, we have to murder perfectionism. I was going to write, "put perfectionism to bed," but that sounded too tender for this particular monster. Murder feels right.

How do we do that? There are a number of ways. Books like *Getting Things Done* by David Allen are great at helping you get organized and in motion. Men's magazines offer monthly tips on productivity with the least effort expended. But I tend to think that the simpler I keep my tools, the more likely I am to actually use them. And there is one idea that really changed the way I looked at perfectionism. Bumping into this truth radically rewired my ability to finish. Here's what I learned: 90 percent perfect and shared with the world always changes more lives than 100 percent perfect and stuck in your head.

That's it. I admit it's simple. But it's also true.

The things you create and share will always out-perform the things that stay stuck in your head or your desk or your laptop. You might love the ideas you have inside you. You might be more proud of them than any other project you've ever put together. But if you don't follow through with them, they don't do much good.

The business that is open will always outsell the business that is closed.

If your goal is to change the world, you have to step out and share your work. And sometimes that means getting comfortable with A-minus work.

I learned that while working on my blog, StuffChristiansLike.net. I used to kill myself on each post. I would write and rewrite each one, trying to perfectly craft what I wanted to say. It's so easy to misinterpret something online and I wanted my message to be clear. It was tempting to hold off on posts until they were perfect.

But 7 a.m. comes at the same time every day. And people expected a post from me. Not a perfect post. A great post. If I wanted to impact someone that day, if I wanted to change the way they thought about something, I had to share what I wrote. Even if I thought it was only 90 percent done. Even if I thought a little more work could make it perfect. Because that's the lie of perfectionism, isn't it?

We never tell ourselves, "The land of perfect is about a year away." We never think perfect is impossible. Perfect always glows from right around the corner. We just need a little more work, a little more time and then we can share our work with the world.

I'm afraid the land of perfect is a myth. We might feel we are skirting its borders with our dream, but the reality is that those borders don't exist because perfect doesn't. Your definition of perfect will not fit mine, which will not fit hers or his. You can't catch perfect. But you can catch published. You can catch finished and shared.

That's not an excuse to do your work halfheartedly. I want you to be excellent at passion, not just passionate. But since industry rules say that the vast majority of us don't read beyond page 18 in books and you've made it this far, chances are good you struggle with perfectionism much more than doing things halfheartedly. The solution to doing something lackadaisically is not difficult. Just do it better. The solution to perfectionism is tricky because at first, it doesn't feel like something that needs to be solved.

At first you get lauded for your "attention to detail" or "commitment to excellence." But what a lot of people don't see are the extra hours you're putting in to make sure something is perfect. Perfectionism seems like a character trait sometimes, not a flaw. People don't normally see it as the poison it is until someone burns out or has a breakdown.

I look at starting any endeavor kind of like swimming. You can read all the books you want about swimming. You can participate in blogs about swimming and buy magazines and study videos of swimming online for hours and hours. But if you waited until you were perfect at understanding swimming before you started swimming, you might never get in the water. And you'd never learn to be a great swimmer, because you have to get wet a lot first.

Quit perfect. It's an unnecessary obstacle. Chase the idea of your dream being better finished at 90 percent than perfect and not pursued.

Death to the discussion

Morning Jon used to hate Night Jon. That's how I thought of each day in my head. When Morning Jon would get up to go to work, he'd be exhausted and worn out before the day even really started. Why? Because Night Jon was an irresponsible jerk. He never thought about anyone but himself. He was always staying up late and watching *The Real World* marathons or reading sports online and then would finally collapse into bed when he was too exhausted to keep his eyes open, thus screwing Morning Jon out of a productive day.

That's how I used to think, mostly because I hated mornings but also because I'm weird. But as tired as I was each morning, there was one thing that wrecked my ability to follow my dream, to move, if you will, each day. It wasn't my lack of sleep or lack of desire. It was the discussion between the other two Jons in my life.

Every time I sat down at my laptop to write my book or my blog, I would have a discussion inside my head. It usually went like this:

Today Jon:
"I think I'll write some today. Today is a good day to hammer out a few ideas!"

Later Jon:
"I agree with you almost. I think you should definitely

write some. You should just do it later. You'll be able to be far more creative and productive later. Do you even feel like writing right now?"

Today Jon:
"I'm a little tired, but yeah, I think I could write today."

Later Jon:
"You should write, but you know, there's a lot of other stuff on your to-do list. There is a load of other obligations you need to take care of first. What if we compromise? You do a few items on your list and then write later."

Today Jon:
"Okay, but I am definitely going to write a ton later!"

Later Jon:
"Without a doubt! We are going to be so productive later!"

Back and forth I went with myself, over and over again, losing the majority of those discussions. Why? Because we know how to talk ourselves out of or into things better than anyone on the planet.

Think about a time when you made a horrible mistake and someone said, "What were you thinking?" Usually you weren't doing it because you thought it would be a horrible mistake. You thought it would be great. And you talked yourself into it. Because no one can convince us like we can convince us.

So when you sit down to do whatever it is you feel called to do, one of the other main obstacles you'll have to face is "the discussion." It's annoying and tricky and sly. It ruins more dreams than just about anything else on the planet, but there is a way to beat it. There is a way to stop it. And the best way to do that, the best way to crush the discussion, is with a decision.

If your desire is to read one book on parenting every week because your dream is being the best parent possible, decide on a time to do that. Decide that every morning at 7:00, you'll read for thirty minutes. And decide that once for the entire month.

Then on day four when doubt creeps in and the discussion fires up, say to yourself, "Oh, I wish you had been around earlier. We already decided to read at 7 a.m. I'd love to discuss this with you, but we've already made our decision. Thanks."

Like an unruly employee at a store who says, "Sorry. I just work here," you then get back to work. You write or read or jog or do a million other things that are no longer up for discussion.

You might need to do this every day at first. We all get a little addicted to the discussion because it keeps us from being brave. We get comfortable with losing to the discussion over and over again. Victory will feel a little weird at first.

But the goal is to make your decision once a month and then once a year. The energy and time you'll save not spent tangling in the discussion can be dramatic. Discussing whether or not to create something each day is exhausting. Each time you lose, it gets a little harder to win next time.

So decide once. And then just do it.

Death to the discussion obstacle.

The fuzzy math of "what if?"

Secretly, I always thought I could be a writer.

That was a passion that I always felt I was capable of executing on. And I really felt that way strongly because I had never tried.

There was nothing to prove me wrong. I had a head full of imagination and a life devoid of experiences that told me otherwise. I used to smugly read book reviews or see people online who had written books and followed my same dream and think to myself, *I could do that, if I really wanted to.*

It is such a toxic phrase: "If I really wanted to."

It's a Get Out Jail Free card. It's not my lack of ability that is holding me back—it's my lack of desire. I could be awesome, if I really wanted to. I could run a marathon, if I really wanted to. I could go back to school, if I really wanted to. We say that phrase when we want to shift the blame for our dream not coming true. It's not that we can't; it's that we won't, and *won't* is a word that speaks to our will. *Can't*, on the other hand, is a word that speaks to our skill. By saying, "If I really wanted to," we are able to maintain the appearance of having enough skill to follow our dream.

This path eventually leads to a curious place—apathy.

Apathy seems like a good friend at times. It's familiar. We've not cared about other things before; why not *not* care about one more thing? It's also much easier than caring. At first. Apathy is almost effortless and grows in quiet places that don't require a lot of tending or maintenance. And for a while, apathy is a lot less terrifying than opportunity.

Apathy is a good friend when an opportunity stares you in the face and you're afraid to actually find out what would happen if you tried to follow through with a dream job or a desire. And it's a good friend because something weird happens when we step out for a big adventure. We start to ask ourselves the "what if" questions.

"What if I try and I fail and it turns out I'm not really a writer after all?"

"What if we have kids and I'm a horrible mother?"

"What if I start my own business and it turns out all these years I've been wrong about being a great entrepreneur?"

In those moments, we become obsessed with the fear of finding out what we are not. It reminds me of how Matt Damon's character describes why he is a murderous imposter in the movie *The Talented Mr. Ripley*. He says, "I always thought it'd be better to be a fake somebody than a real nobody." Apathy is ultimately about being a "fake somebody."[8]

We're afraid of finding out what we're really made of so instead we end up making no decision because neutral is safe. We think that if we don't do anything, we won't make the wrong decision. But not doing anything is its own decision, and the odds of failure are horrible.

Let's pretend that you decide to pursue your dream job with all your heart. Let's say that, like me, you put all the chips in and move your family and change jobs and end relationships and start new ones in a new state. Five years later you look back on the decision and either it worked or it didn't. There will be shades of differentiation in there, but for the most part you'll either have succeeded (you made the right decision) or failed (you made the wrong decision). So you have roughly 50 percent odds of things working out.

But nobody fears just making the wrong decision. Through the kaleidoscope we fear the worst possible outcome we can imagine—a series of interrelated failures, a spider web of screw-ups that collapses our entire being. When I play that game, I go from "mistake" to "hobo on the streets" in about five minutes. I imagine losing my job in some sort of spectacular way that prevents me from ever finding gainful employment again. I don't just get blacklisted in one industry; I manage to get barred from every industry on the planet. My family would leave me too because I'd be a hobo and they wouldn't want to be part of my new drifter lifestyle. Riding the rails and whatnot. I'd kick around the Pacific Northwest and try to become a glassblower or something, but that wouldn't work either.

Ultimately I'd fall apart and people would use me as a cautionary tale of extreme potential gone to extreme waste.

The chances of that happening, of you or me really wasting our lives to that degree, are very, very slim. They're probably 1 percent. Maybe 2 percent if you already know a guy who's into glassblowing and lives in the Pacific Northwest.

Now let's say that your fear of answering "What if?" is massive. You're paralyzed by it and in order to avoid it you don't make any decision about pursuing your dream. You now have a 100 percent chance of your dream not coming to fruition. People who do not attempt to recover their dreams fail 100 percent of the time.

So you have a 2 percent chance of horrific failure if you try and a 100 percent chance if you don't. Those are horrible odds, but maybe I overexaggerated and 2 percent is incredibly low. Let's pretend there's a 50 percent chance that your worst failure comes to fruition. Those odds are still better than not trying at all.

You might fail. By recovering your dream and running with it, risk runs with you. You could fall flat on your face. But I'd accept that risk a thousand times before I accepted the guarantee of failure of not trying.

Do the math and don't make the fear of failure an insurmountable obstacle.

We are too busy to pursue our dreams

I make it a point not to complain about my life around people who have more than five kids. If you have one

of those economy vans that prisons use to transfer con-
victs and if you have established a precise system to put on
shoes at your house, chances are good you are busier than
I am.

I didn't realize this principle until we had our second
kid and discovered that having two kids is exponentially
harder than having one. Don't get me wrong; when we
had our first daughter, L.E., I thought we were busy. I'm
sure I complained to people about being deprived of sleep
and overworked. But then we had a second kid and things
got crazy. Suddenly we went from zone defense to man-
to-man. That's when we got busy. But that's okay, because
busy is a bit of a badge of honor these days.

And so many of us wear that badge. And we are busy.
We work longer hours than previous generations. Harvard
economist Juliet B. Schor, in her book *The Overworked
American*, estimates that "the average employed person is
now on the job an additional 163 hours, or the equivalent
of one month a year, compared to figures from twenty years
ago."[9] And trying to fit a dream into that already rabid
schedule seems impossible, if not foolish.

So we comfort ourselves by saying, "I'd pursue my
dream if I had time."

I wrestled with that excuse when I wrote my first book.
I wasn't the first person to turn a blog into a book. In fact,
my inspiration, Christian Lander, had already turned his
blog Stuff White People Like into one. So had a lot of other
bloggers, and there was a bit of a pattern established.

Sign huge book deal. Quit job. Stop writing blog for a while. Hole yourself up in a moody-looking apartment. Write book.

But I didn't receive a massive advance. I couldn't quit my 40-hour-a-week job. On top of that, I had freelance clients for whom I had to write dozens of projects. I had two kids who were not about to accept a parenting hiatus for three months while I worked on a book. And the most difficult part was that I couldn't stop writing my blog. So every day I had to double the amount of content I was creating, writing a post for the blog and a chapter of the book.

I was busy.

So are you.

You've got commitments and jobs and kids and a dog and a spouse or significant other. You've got in-laws or neighbors and a BlackBerry that won't shut up and morning meetings and lunchtime workouts and evening commitments. You've got a second or maybe even a third job and into that maelstrom, some punk kid who turned a blog into a book is telling you you're not too busy to chase your dream.

Only that's not what I'm saying. I believe you're busy, I do. But there's something I believe even more.

You have the perfect amount of time each day for the things that matter most. The key is spending time on those things.

Few would boldly declare, "Today, watching television for two hours was one of the most important things

I needed to get done." Yet that's where we sometimes spend our entire evenings. The operative word in the phrase "enough time" is not *time*. It's *enough*. And the truth you should accept is that you will probably never have "enough" time to pursue your dream. But every day somebody somewhere is making magic with the less-than-enough time he has. So can you, if you stop focusing on the amount of time you have and start focusing on the amount of tasks that really matter.

You will never happen upon a productivity tip that increases your ability to get things done so dramatically that you have too much time on your hands. You might be too bored to work on your dream, but just don't buy into the lie that you are too busy.

The money problem

It kills me when I hear people equating financial foolishness with being committed to their dream.

"We decided to go for broke. We canceled Christmas for a couple years and sold our kids' toys in a big garage sale. We then pawned my wife's wedding ring. Finally, we lost our house. That's how much the dream meant to me."

That's ridiculous. Mortgaging your future isn't a sign of faithfulness to a dream; it's a sign of foolishness. If you're not careful and buy into the lie that in order to "go for broke," you have to "go broke," you'll turn your dream into a demon. Money will become a high-walled border around your dream if you don't control it. It will limit what you can do and when you can do it, like a barbed-wire fence at a prison. If you can control it though, money can be a strong, stable place to jump from.

I experienced both sides of the equation.

When I was young, I made really stupid decisions with money. I took out a loan to buy a mountain bike. I forgot to pay a health care bill that went to collections and wrecked my credit for years. I bought an expensive new car and had no savings plan whatsoever. Years later, the collective mistakes caught up with me.

I was unable to work on my dream for years because I needed to take freelance writing jobs in addition to my day job in order to get out from the hole I dug. I lost the freedom to say no and had to take on some less-than-perfect clients. I wanted to write books and work on dream projects, but my weeknights and weekends were filled with freelance work.

Eventually, years after reading my employer's book *The Total Money Makeover* and hustling on freelance, we got rid of our credit cards. We paid off our car loan. We paid off item after item until only our home mortgage remained. I didn't know it at the time, but we weren't just paying our bills; we were removing financial obstacles from the runway of our dream.

When we did so, money became something that didn't prevent our dream but actually funded it. We had saved enough to take low-paying speaking gigs in order to get better at speaking. We had enough in the bank for me to say no to freelance projects that would have eaten up dream time.

Money is certainly a legitimate obstacle to your ability to pursue your dream job, but it doesn't have to be. I'm biased because I work for Dave Ramsey and love the *Financial Peace University* classes, but regardless of the path you take, get control of your finances if you really want the freedom to pursue your dream well. If you approach money the right way now, it will fund and fuel your dream, not curb it.

Two of the worst words ever

I hate the words *by now*. Not separately. I've never had a problem with *by* when it's on its own or supporting another sentence. I have no issue with "Stuff Christians Like, *by* Jon Acuff." It performs admirably in that example. And *now* is a fine word too. Short, rhymes with *cow*, often the place people encourage you to live. I got nothing but love for *now*.

But when those two words team up and hit the town together, fist pumping and drinking the night away, they become something entirely different. They are not peanut butter and chocolate, together at last. They are orange juice and gasoline, helpful in isolation, napalm collectively.

The problem is that "by now" is a phrase we say to ourselves when we're trying to believe the lie that it's too late to start pursuing our dream. As we survey our lives and stand on the edge of the possibility cliff, we start to say things like:

"If I were really going to be a high school teacher, by now I would have already had a few years of teaching experience."

"If I were going to be a musician, by now I'd be better at the guitar."

"If I were going to be a pastor, by now I would have gone to seminary."

The goal of the phrase "by now" is to offer yourself a twisted justification that, indeed, you could have been what you wanted to be but, alas, you're too late. The tricky thing is that "by now" isn't age-specific. You'll tell yourself this at 25 or 55.

And if you convince yourself of this, you will also believe the next lie, which is "Don't start."

The window of opportunity has closed. The ship has sailed while I was busy working or parenting or paying off student loans. It's too late. Don't start.

Don't let the phrase "by now" in. Like the vampires in the first Corey Haim film, *Lost Boys* (the only *Lost Boys* film I officially recognize), it can only come in if you invite it.

What if I do the wrong thing?

I wish there were a chapter in this book entitled "Wicked Big Confidence" and it was easier to write than this one about obstacles. But it wouldn't be true to my experience. And if it were true of yours and you were already brimming with a billboard-sized belief in your abilities and a perfect plan for your dream, you probably wouldn't be reading this book. You'd be on a yacht with Carmen Electra, a wheelbarrow of Lucky Charms and a full-size Galaga arcade machine. (That is what I assumed would happen for me when I was in the ninth grade.)

But the fear of doing what we're called to do comes in a Baskin Robbins assortment of disgusting flavors and one of them is the question, "What if I do the wrong thing?"

I'm working through that one right now. Seven months ago, I left the stability of an IT job at a massive company in Atlanta. It wasn't speeding me in the direction of my dream job but it was consistent and safe. I loved my boss and the people I worked with. I had a steady salary and got to do a lot of the stuff I dreamed about on the side of my job, in the corners of life. Openly I questioned what it would be like to do what I love full time, but not enough to actually do something about it.

Then Dave Ramsey pulled me aside and made me a ridiculous offer. I had just finished speaking to his team of roughly 300 people at a weekly meeting. I'd driven up from Atlanta, expecting to maybe have a casual meeting with one of his team leaders about doing some freelance work. My expectations were low.

After I was done speaking, Dave asked me to stick around and have a conversation. I consider him a celebrity but still tried to play it cool and act like I regularly had big conversations like this in fancy conference rooms with comfortable chairs. My cover was almost blown when Dave's assistant walked in and said, "Dave, you have to call Tony Dungy in five minutes." Now that I'm a thousandaire, I'd probably say, "Tell Dungy we'll call him back later. He's not even an active NFL coach anymore." But those were humbler days back then, and I physically constrained myself from letting out an audible, "Whoa!"

Dave told me he was looking for new message bearers with new messages. He wanted to find people he could pour decades of leadership wisdom into. This wasn't a job offer; this was a long-term dream job offer, a chance to do what I've always wanted to do with my life. The opportunity to write the things I want to write and speak at the places I want to speak and follow my dream like never before.

So I took him up on his offer. At the time of this writing, I've been with Dave for the last seven months. And despite a successful book release under my belt, *Gazelles, Baby Steps And 37 Other Things Dave Ramsey Taught Me About Debt*, a dozen fun speaking engagements behind me, and the best months I've ever spent at a job, fear still exists. Particularly the fear that I might have done the wrong thing and made the wrong decision.

I moved my family from Atlanta to Nashville. My daughter L.E. will start second grade at the third school she's attended. My wife left her core group of friends she'd known for years. I left a really steady job and a whole host of freelance clients. I left my literary agent, who was amazing, and my original publisher, who was great as well.

I left a lot behind, and the fear that I might have made the wrong decision still pops up. What if something horrible happens and I lose this job? I have no agent. No publisher. No job, and a family stuck in a state we don't really know. Perhaps even worse, I might have spent years chasing one thing only to realize that it was the wrong thing to pursue. I will have wasted years of my life traveling down the wrong path.

It would be easy for me to feel that way about my career in advertising. The goal of an advertising career is to get a job at a big agency in a big city with big clients. I am 0 for 3 at that goal. I never once rode a scooter through an office or worked on a Super Bowl campaign or created a viral video that millions saw. More than that, my only experience with a real ad agency was getting my portfolio dissected by Mark while my mother-in-law waited for me in the parking lot.

The worst part is that I used to kid myself that I was in advertising. At AutoTrader.com I would tell myself, "Any written words on a website are part of the brand experience for a customer, which makes what I write branding, which means I am technically in advertising." But the truth is that AutoTrader.com had a marketing department and I was not in it. I was in IT. I didn't really write advertising, I wrote instructional copy, like: "Please enter a correct five-digit zip code into the field." There were certainly shades of branding involved in some projects, and I sometimes got to write banner ads, but for the most part I was not in advertising.

What a waste of twelve years I'll never have my dream is to write books, then I just spent a dozen years going down the wrong path. It's easy to think that way. But is it the truth?

Six years ago, author Donald Miller told me something. I let him know I wanted to write books but was kind of floundering in advertising. With a kindness I did not deserve or understand at the time, he said, "Your career in advertising is important. It's a great way to learn how to encourage people to do things. That's a skill that will really serve you well when you start to write books."

He was right. My years were not wasted in advertising. Those years became fodder for my dream job, the raw materials of life I needed back then to do what I am doing right now.

I know sometimes it's scary to think that you might do the wrong thing. It's terrifying to imagine wasting your "one shot." But let me assure you, nothing you do will be wasted. Every decision you make, every path you take, has the ability to contribute something you need to succeed at your dream.

Tony Robbins, whom I probably couldn't dunk on, says, "Your greatest resource is resourcefulness." It's just a matter of seeing it that way. After a frustrating, seemingly unsuccessful twelve years, I no longer see my advertising career as a waste. It's a resource that continues to fuel my dream with real-life experience, real-life hopes and real-life stories.

And that's exactly the kind of fuel your dream needs too.

It would be easier if _____

There are a bajillion ways to fill in that blank. We already discussed time constraints but when it comes to making excuses not to pursue our dream, we often create a fictional set of conditions that must occur for us to move. We create them because then we can feel better about currently wussing out. The funny thing is that we tend to say things we know we can't really do much about.

"It would be easier if I didn't have a full-time job."

"It would be easier if I didn't have kids."

"It would be easier if I had a wealthy relative who could bankroll me."

"It would be easier if I weren't married."

Those are a few of the excuses I heard in my head when I started to write my first book and they were senseless because I couldn't easily do anything about them other than complain and waste energy.

"It would be easier if I didn't have a full-time job."

We always assume that more free time will equal more productivity but often that isn't true. I personally tend to get more done when I am busy. But let's pretend that wasn't the case. Even if more time did equal more book writing, I wouldn't be able to pay my bills. We weren't living lavishly when I got serious about my personal writing, but it turns out the hospital requires money for their services. So does the grocery store. And the mortgage company. So wishing that I didn't have a full-time job was a stupid complaint. I had to make money somewhere, and Lowe's had run out of the trees that grow it. Move on.

"It would be easier if I didn't have kids."

You know how many books I was able to write in all my free time before kids? Zero. But parents often blame their inability to pursue their dreams on their kids. That's a fun cycle of shame and guilt to get on. Regret not following your dream. Blame your kids because you're busy. Feel guilty for blaming your kids and not loving them as much as other parents who don't blame their kids. Give up on your dream for a little while. Eventually regret not following your dream again. Repeat. This one is even dumber than complaining about not having a job because I had kids. I could always quit my job. I should never quit my kids.

"It would be easier if I had a wealthy relative who could bankroll me."

My dad is a pastor. Back when I was a kid, pastors didn't drive Rolls-Royces. (It's possible he was too lazy, but I feel it might have been a moral decision on his part. Hard to say.) I didn't grow up wealthy. I used to be terrified that my mom would ask us to rock the Knights of the Round Table shirts instead of real Polo shirts, which we couldn't really afford. We were by no means poor, but none of the minivans my mom drove ever had spinning rims. Wishing you were born into money or somehow had more of your own is a fun excuse because our society is laced with phrases like, "You need to spend money to make money" and, "Money makes the world go round." So if you were rich or your parents set you up with a trust fund, maybe it would be easier to do your dream. But guess what?

I've never read the biography of someone successful that had a chapter titled "The Day I Found the Bag of Diamonds." And let's be honest—do the rich people you see in the tabloids always seem happy and content? Have you ever seen a cover of *US* that says, "Ten years of no celebrities entering rehab; they're all too busy living their dreams!" Usually it's the other way around. Money can't buy happiness, a thought I just came up with on my own and should probably trademark. And although I've met some happy, hardworking wealthy people, I've also met some incredibly miserable wealthy people too. Don't wait for money to save you.

"It would be easier if I weren't married."

This one is ridiculous because I know it would have been impossible to ever write a book without my wife's support. You personally might be able to change the world at a young age, but I was really immature. The younger, single version of me was incapable of the discipline to sit down and actually do something meaningful. So fantasizing that my marriage is somehow preventing my dream is just dumb. If you find yourself spending much time on this excuse, chances are your dream is not the only thing that's suffering in your life. It's a gross excuse, but I've honestly made this one before and when I did, it was during a time when my wife and I were in a really bad spot in our marriage. We ended up going to counseling and spending a lot of time on our marriage before I could even worry about my dream. If you're there in your marriage, get some help. (And if you do, don't try to guess what the other people are "in here for" in the counselor's lobby. Apparently folks don't like that.)

A spouse needs to be on the same page with you and a partner in what you are chasing. You never want to have them on the other side of your dream because the harder you lean into it, the further away you'll push them. Looking back on it, there's absolutely no way my first book would have ever seen the light of day without my wife's constant support, encouragement and love.

I'm not sure what your excuse is. Maybe you've never thought, *It would be easier if* _____, but chances are you've wasted time before spinning out on something that is never going to be. You can't go back and be born to a wealthier dad. You've got to be a mom or dad to your own kids. In most cases you have to work. And if you're in a marriage that can be healthy but has hit a bump in the road, getting a divorce is not going to lead to instant dream fulfillment.

Let go of "It would be easier if _____."

Less risk, more reward

There are thousands of possible risks and I only covered a handful. Even if you get great at looking at them, even if you develop the best telescope on the planet, that won't eliminate risk completely. The only people who don't face risk are dead people, and they don't buy books or at least aren't in our target audience, so I'm going to ignore the needs of the dead. The undead too while I'm at it.

But there are ways to mitigate the risks you'll face as you pursue your dream job. There are methods to neutralize financial risks and personal risks and professional risks as you step out in your dream. There are tricks you can learn to shrink the risks you'll see along the way. And the surprising thing is that you can find those tips in the last place most dreamers look.

Your day job.

CHAPTER 4

Falling in Like With a Job You Don't Love

For the first ten years I held a day job, I thought about quitting at least once a week. I'd often wake up counting the number of remaining days I had to get up early that week. I'd run quitter's math in my head, playing out possible scenarios. *If I stay at AutoTrader.com until 2009, I will have been here over two years, which will look better on my résumé and give me something to say to my wife when she observes, "You always quit your job so fast." "Not true," I'll say. "I stayed at AutoTrader.com for two years."*

Every time I'd attend an annual team meeting, I'd think, *This is probably my last one.* When project deadlines would be extended, I'd imagine never seeing the end of the project. I'd be long gone by then.

I've always obsessed about quitting my job. Then something weird happened in 2008. People started encouraging me to quit. Not because I had a bad attitude or they were sick of my performance. People were urging me to quit my job because I started to dream.

The relationship between dream jobs and day jobs is so misunderstood in our culture that we think success at one means the instant death of the other. So when I signed a book contract in 2008 and saw my blog start blowing up, people came out of the woodwork to ask, "When are you going to quit your job?"

With a degree of incredulousness that bordered on stupor, friends and family expressed shock at my sanity. "Why haven't you quit yet? Why are you still there?" In a culture of quitters we assume dumping the day job is the first step when the dream starts to stick. Have dream. Have small modicum of success. Quit job.

People asked me this constantly when I wrote my first book. They were so excited for me because surely it was going to happen soon. I was going to fulfill the great American dream. I was going to quit my day job!

Even my boss regularly asked how long I was going to be at my job now that I had a book deal. She poked and prodded, often in a joking way, but she was not the only executive who said I "wouldn't be around for long."

This is tempting. When enough people ask when you're quitting, you start to feel dumb for staying. If one of our culture's definitions of success is to dump your day job, then staying at one can make you feel like a failure.

Part of the reason people encouraged me to quit is that they assumed my dream was more lucrative than it was. Many people assume authors are paid a tremendous amount of money when they publish a book. Thanks to folks like Stephen King and J. K. Rowling, the general public believes that when you write a book you get to wear platinum pants with a diamond fly. Thus far, not my experience.

The truth is I got a $30,000 advance for my first book. After taxes, my literary agent's fee and a 10 percent tithe, I got about $13,000. Right, but what about royalties? The reality is that 95 percent of authors never see a dime of royalties. You have to sell back your entire advance before you earn a dollar of your royalty. The first sales report I got from the publisher did not include a check. It was a statement that said I was $15,000 in the hole. I got a piece of paper that literally said my books had earned negative $15,000.

People don't realize this, and so they still asked when I was going to quit. In order to respond, I had to reframe the entire conversation.

I found the lottery example helpful. When friends would pester me about quitting, I would tell them I walked away from my publishing deal with thirteen grand. I'd then say, "If you won $13,000 in the lottery, would you quit your job?" Of course not. No one would ever say, "I'm out of here. Me and my thirteen Gs are moving to Mexico!"

If that example didn't work, I'd tell people how much my dream paid hourly. Dreams rarely pay well at first. In the first four years I consistently wrote a blog, a publisher paid me $13,000 for about 2,300 hours of writing. That's about $5.65 per hour. The federal minimum wage is currently $7.25. At the time I could have earned more working at Starbucks than I could writing a book in Starbucks.

But the money issue is only one small, small part of the reason I stayed at my day job nearly two years after I received my book contract. Money mattered, but it wasn't the main issue.

The real reason I stayed at AutoTrader.com is that if I had quit my day job too soon I would have killed my dream job.

The incubation of a dream

How long does it take for your dream to become a full-time job and sustain you?

Longer than you want it to.

I don't know the exact answer for you, but every dream takes longer than you want it to. Our time frame is always shorter and faster than what a dream has in mind. And if we rush it, if we don't give it time to incubate, we usually end up killing it before it even has a chance to breathe.

The year 2008 was a crazy year for me. On March 21, I started StuffChristiansLike.net, which instantly exploded into a global platform. That fall, Zondervan offered me a book deal. I also got invited to speak at Dave Ramsey's organization.

I'd only spoken professionally once before I drove to Nashville to address the entire staff of about 300 people. I was nervous because I knew they'd recently had a famous musician come in and do the same thing. I made a joke about that during my speech. At the end, they all gave me a standing ovation and Dave Ramsey said from stage, "That famous musician didn't get a standing ovation." (I'd say his name but he lives in Nashville near me and is apparently working out a lot these days.) After a tour of the building, I walked to my car on cloud nine. A member of their web team chased me down in the parking lot and said, "Jon, what would you think about working here? We've got a web copywriting position open that I think you might be perfect for."

I remember calling my wife on the drive home to Atlanta and telling her that we were probably going to move to Nashville soon! We both called our parents and shared the exciting news. Inside, I thought, *This is it! Finally, my dream of not working a day job is coming to fruition. It's all coming together! I'm going to quit AutoTrader.com.*

That was a "this is it" crossroads moment. When we fantasize about how our dreams will come to life, we often think of them like this: We're walking by a football field when a ball lands at our feet. The coach yells, "Hey kid, throw that ball back." In a moment of profound dexterity, we unleash a perfect 60-yard spiral into the end zone and the waiting arms of a shocked receiver. The coach drops his clipboard in astonishment and we start our first NFL game that Sunday. We've been discovered!

But I'm pretty sure that's not how most dreams work, despite Hollywood's efforts. I think there are certainly exciting moments when an opportunity vaults you over a number of hurdles, but in general I think they take longer than that. Mine did.

I didn't end up taking that job from the Ramsey team in the fall of 2008. Months later I turned down another position. Over a two-year period, I spoke at three companywide meetings before finally accepting my dream job in the summer of 2010 when Dave approached me personally. But let's pretend that I did accept that first opportunity.

I would have come on board as a web copywriter. It's a great position and one I've done in some form or the other for ten years of my career. I would have loved the team and the work would have been more fulfilling than other jobs I had. But by accepting that job and declaring myself a web copywriter, I would have forever killed the dream job I ended up with at Dave Ramsey.

The job they offered me in 2010 was essentially to be a full-time speaker and a full-time author. After watching me grow my brand, platform and dream for two years, they were confident it was a mission they wanted to support.

It's unlikely I would have arrived at the same place had I taken a job as a web copywriter. They would have been supportive of Stuff Christians Like, but it would have been impossible for them to see me as someone they could mold into a new message bearer if instead of patiently growing my dream I had spent two years telling them I was a web copywriter. I would have quit my job at AutoTrader.com and ruined my dream before it had fully grown into what it is now.

AutoTrader.com gave me time to slowly incubate my dream. To make mistakes that didn't cost too much and try new things with much smaller risks. Although I had written online before, I didn't know what a blog was when I started there in 2006. By the time I left, my dream had become something big and powerful and true. My dream had a fighting chance because it spent time maturing while I held on to my day job.

I'm not the only one who had a day job while chasing a dream job either. Turns out a guy named Leonardo da Vinci did too. In the book *How to Think Like Leonardo da Vinci*, author Michael J. Gelb talked about how da Vinci often had to serve as a party planner for the patrons who sponsored him. He wrote, "It's amazing to imagine a genius of da Vinci's stature devoting his time to the design of pageants, balls, costumes and other ephemerae, yet as Kenneth Clark points out, 'This was expected of Renaissance artists between Madonnas.'"[10]

Leonardo da Vinci, widely regarded as one of the greatest artists who ever lived, worked a day job while he pursued his passion. Chances are you will, too, but that doesn't mean it has to be miserable.

I think we do a tremendous disservice to our dream jobs when we talk about pursuing them to the detriment of our day jobs. If a dream is going to take us ten months or ten years to realize, we can't accept heartache or horror forty hours a week. It's the "platform and the prison" principle. If you're patient and deliberate, your day job can become a wonderful platform from which you can launch your dream job. If you demonize your day job though and rail against it, it becomes a prison you'll try to escape from. And prison breaks rarely go well for anyone.

The truth is, we need to learn to fall in like with a job we don't love because it's actually the best way to set up your dream for success.

What does your dream have to do with your job?

We like to pretend sometimes that we are made up of a system of buckets. We like to think we can live "What happens in Vegas, stays in Vegas" moments in one area of our lives without affecting the other areas. It's just not true. If you're ailing in one portion of your life, it tends to infect the other portions. If there's poison in a glass of water, no one says, "Be careful, the *middle* of that water is poisoned."

The same principle applies to your work. Bad employees make horrible dreamers. You can't loaf on your day job all week and then expect to magically throw the switch on the weekend and hustle on your dream. The things you do on your day job tend to follow you home.

I didn't believe this until I started to actively change the way I behaved in meetings. I was having a hard time listening at home. As soon as my wife would start saying anything I didn't find interesting, I would tune out. I've never been a great listener, but this was getting out of hand.

One day in a meeting at AutoTrader.com, I realized what was going on.

Every week, five days a week, I was checking out in meetings. Most of the meetings I went to did not have earth-shaking implications for my life, so in a lot of them I got bored. I would daydream about things I wanted to do, run through my personal to-do list, or try to think what my favorite word might be. (I settled on a tie between *nougat* and *bungalow*).

Then, after hours and hours of not listening to other people talk, I would go home and act surprised that it was difficult to listen to my wife. It was happening because for forty hours a week, I was training myself not to pay attention to people. It was happening because we are whole people and can't separate ourselves into "buckets."

That's the biggest reason it's critical you work hard at your day job. You're not just working; you're practicing for your dream. Even if they're completely unrelated, and I'm not sure they are, the effort you invest in work will return big dividends to your dream. If you want your dream job to work, work on your day job.

Remember why you work

I have what dentists call "lottery mouth." I don't technically know if they've ever used this phrase, but they should. Because when dentists look inside my mouth, they envision ski boats and second homes and college tuition for their kids.

I've got fillings to be replaced, cavities from having braces three different times and an endless gold mine of wisdom teeth to extract. And the day before a big speaking event one year, I even had an emergency root canal.

It started at 4 in the morning. Waves of pain every forty minutes. The right side of my face would turn gray, one eye would go red, and I would enter a small space in my head where my dying tooth would scream, "There is no pain in this dojo!" But there was pain in that dojo, oh there was. I went to work and tried to tough it out. I scheduled an appointment with a root canal specialist and then set my stopwatch to 24 hours because that's how long I had to make it.

By the time my appointment rolled around, I wanted to front hug the dentist I was so happy to be there. I was moments away from freedom, I was on the edge of relief and I was ecstatic.

But it didn't quite go the way I thought it would.

Ninety minutes into the procedure, I was still in agonizing pain. Apparently I have roller-coaster roots that flip and turn inside my teeth. The dentist couldn't use just an electric tool to kill them. Instead he had to also use hand tools and slowly twist his way with a long thin file into tiny holes he had drilled into my teeth. Imagine someone spinning a titanium needle back and forth between their thumb and index finger deep inside your tooth for an hour and a half.

I asked for more Novocain. Based on the pain I was in, I figured the dentist would say, "Sure, hook up this

Camelbak hydration system and drink it through a straw. Have all you want. It's pineapple flavor; you'll love it."

Instead, he said, "I can't give you any more. I've already reached the limit of what you can handle. If I give you any more, your vision will blur."

My first thought was, "For how long? I'm not reading a book right now. I'll get a cab to take me home. Are you saying my vision will blur forever or just for a few hours? I promise, I don't need perfect vision for the rest of this day. I'm not performing any open-heart surgeries. Give me the Novocain."

He wasn't budging. So I sat there with bolts of electricity shooting through the nerve highway of my mouth. I thought I had reached the worst point until I felt a hygienist place something small in my hand. *Did that really just happen?* I thought to myself. *Did a hygienist just place a ball in my hand to squeeze because it's about to get even worse? What century am I in? I'm not getting a Pancho Villa bullet removed on a battlefield right now. A ball? Seriously? Is there a strap of leather I can bite down on too? Just go ahead and give me a shot of whiskey while you're at it and heat up a blacksmith's iron to cauterize the wound.*

On that day, driving home from the endodontist's office, it was not difficult to understand why I worked. I had purpose and motivation to continue being an awesome employee. I would have worked at a sewage plant that day if it meant I could pay for my mouth demon to be exorcised.

We forget those things sometimes, though. We get really focused on our own stuff and our own dreams and we lose sight of the many, many reasons it is critical that you do great work at your day job.

That's why, as I write this, I am wearing a Silly Band.

I have two little daughters. And although sometimes Silly Bandz are used as currency at our house much the same way cigarettes are used in prison, they help me remember one of the big reasons I work.

I work so that my kids can eat and wear clothes and sleep indoors.

Sometimes I forget things like that. In the midst of chasing my dreams, I can get lost in being selfish and self-serving. I act like I'm the captain of my own planet and my actions only impact me. There's a wild amount of self-confidence needed to successfully chase a dream, and it's easy for that to mutate into pride and arrogance.

So it might be good to remind yourself why you're working. And that's not an exercise that only moms and dads can go through. Regardless of whether you have kids, it's good to reconnect to the often-quiet reasons you actually go into work.

BE HONEST. WHEN IS THE LAST TIME YOU THOUGHT TO YOURSELF:

1. I'll be able to eat this week because I went to work.

2. I'll be able to sleep out of the rain this week because I worked.

3. I'll get to wear shoes today because I have a job.

4. If I break my pelvis, I will have the insurance to pay for it.

5. I will not have to canal my own roots because I work.

6. I'll be able to support a nonprofit organization because I work.

Those apply to everyone, not just parents or spouses. Take five minutes and write down all the reasons you really work. The better you know them, the easier it will be for you to fall in like with a job you don't love. And if you're having a tough time coming up with them, try these methods.

Look for parallels

A year ago I spent almost every morning of the week writing satirical observations about church and Christianity. I spent almost every day of the week writing technical copy for an IT company. In the mornings I would blog, "Please don't interlink digits with me at church if the minister asks us to hold hands. I don't know you that well, stranger, and it makes me feel like we're going to make out." In the afternoons I would write the two-word label, "Credit Center."

That was how I spent a good deal of my job, writing labels and error messages and instructions on how to use a financial calculator. It was not glamorous work. It was not the fountain of creativity I might have been looking for, but there was a direct parallel.

It was not difficult to see that learning to write with brevity and clarity at work provided direct benefits to my ability to write with brevity and clarity at home. But what if you work at Starbucks and want to be a songwriter? What if you work at a Starbucks and you want to be a CPA and open up your own business? Or you're a stay-at-home mom and you miss the work you used to do in an office? Where are the parallels there?

Let's look at some of those examples.

We'll go ahead and take the Starbucks barista versus songwriter discussion off the table. If you want to write songs and you are surrounded by people and stories all day in one of the most communal places on the planet and you still can't see the connection, you're probably not going to make a good songwriter.

Instead, let's look at Starbucks barista versus CPA. If we sat down to talk about the parallels between those two, here is what I would tell you:

1. **Starbucks is going to teach you about money.**
   That's what being a CPA is all about. You will handle hundreds of dollars a day as a barista. What patterns do you see? What math is present in simple economic transactions? When does the manager balance the books? If this Starbucks was one of your clients, what

sort of accounting grade would you give them? If you were going to analyze the financial health of this location, where would you start?

2. Starbucks is going to teach you about people.
As a CPA, you will have clients. What do you do at Starbucks to delight your customers? How did the people who are regulars become regulars? What have been some customer service mistakes you've made that would cost you ten times that amount of business if you made them as a CPA? What qualities does Starbucks look for in managers? Could those be the same qualities you look for in employees you might hire some day?

3. Starbucks is going to teach you about marketing.
Coffee is cutthroat and the economy has made things even harder. How has Starbucks responded with marketing? Does your location get involved in the community? What would be the grassroots version of an expensive marketing campaign Starbucks did? How could you adapt it?

The parallels go on. But again, maybe that example is too easy. Let's talk about stay-at-home moms.

You've got two kids under the age of six. We're not talking about finding parallels between two salaried jobs. We're talking about finding parallels between a 24-hour-a-day job and, let's say, a desire to be a project manager again.

My wife was a project manager at both an ad agency
and a construction company. Let's say she came to me one
day and said, "Jon, I can't do this anymore. I want to be a
mom and a project manager again. But those aren't related
at all, and I don't see any possible parallels."

THREE QUESTIONS I WOULD ASK HER AND YOU:

1. **Why?**
   That's usually the best question to start with. I would
   first and foremost want to know why my wife wanted
   to be a project manager again. Maybe she didn't want
   the job back, she just wanted to feel in community with
   other people. Maybe it wasn't about the specifics of the
   industry but instead about feeling like you're responsible
   for something outside the house. If that's the case, then
   we can look for a million freelance opportunities and
   not just limit ourselves to construction companies and
   ad agencies.

2. **How much time can you give it?**
   It only generates obscene amounts of hurt and frustration to pursue a 40-hour-a-week dream in a week
   that currently has four hours of available free time. It's
   useless to talk about finding the parallels between a
   full-time job and being a stay-at-home mom if you've
   only got a few hours in a week to dedicate to it. Instead, for now, scale down your discussion and make

sure you're not comparing apples and oranges. Compare your stay-at-home parenting to a part-time freelance gig if you're not ready to jump in with both feet. Otherwise you won't make a fair comparison.

3. **How can you start small?**
    This is the golden age of freelance. In the 1950s, you couldn't go online, find a quick-hit freelance job, knock it out at home, and feel good about completing a new project while keeping your eye on the kids. Find ways to start small. I would tell my wife that she should start reading blogs from project managers. She's been out of the field for more than six years. Thinking she can jump back in without at least a minor degree of re-education would be crazy. I'd tell her to read the freelance posts on Craigslist to see if there are any small parallels between how she currently spends her days and the ways people are requiring freelance gigs be completed. I would help her go small long before I would help her go big.

I didn't mention the parallels between a day job and a dream job that involve an office, because most of them are obvious. Regardless of the specifics of the two office jobs you are comparing, you will need to be amazing in meetings at both jobs. You will need to have a well-oiled communication system. You will need to build a network of relationships internally so you can get stuff done and externally so you can foster the brand—your own or your company's.

The parallels are endless in most situations. But let's pretend they're not in your world. There are absolutely no parallels between your day job and dream job.

How do you fall in like with a day job like that?

You look instead for purpose.

The purpose filter

Dreams jobs and day jobs are two-way streets. When you look for parallels between your day job and your dream job, you're usually looking in one direction. You're asking, "How can this job impact my dream?" But the things you learn pursuing your dream can also benefit your current job. What happens when you ask, "How can this dream impact my job?"

That's more of a purpose question than a parallel question. Asking it saved me during my two-year incubation at AutoTrader.com.

In the fall of 2009, I used some of my vacation days from work to go speak at conferences around the country. This was an incredibly fun thing to do, but I started to grow bitter about the re-entry process. I was angry about the widening gap between my job and my dream. On one particular morning, I broke down and started crying in the airport. For the record, I cried in the Chicago airport, not the Atlanta airport. And the tears were brief, subtle and related to a pair of khaki pants I didn't want to put back on.

It was 4:30 a.m. and I was walking in O'Hare. Hours earlier, I had spoken to a crowd of hundreds as the closing keynote for a creative conference. Hours later, I would be back at my day job, and the whole thing would feel like it had never happened.

I knew the closer I got to my hometown of Atlanta, the more faded the memory of Chicago would become. The khakis were part of that.

They were hanging in my car in the parking lot at work. After spending twenty-one hours in Chicago, I would fly to Atlanta, ride the train to work, grab my office clothes, and change in the handicap bathroom stall. In a few minutes, I'd transform back into Day Job Guy and disappear in a sea of cubicles.

I didn't want to wear those khakis. I didn't want to do the reverse Superman. I didn't want to jump into the phone booth and put back on normal clothes. *Why can't I do this other thing all the time? Why can't I just quit my day job and be free to pursue my dream job now?*

These thoughts were cascading in my head when I called my wife. "I'm here. I landed. I'm safe. I'm going to ride the train and change clothes. I'm going to stop being Superman."

Without missing a beat she replied, "Superman needed Clark Kent. Being Clark was the reason he was able to be Superman. It was how he stayed real, how he connected to real people. He couldn't be Superman the whole time. He knew the problems of the day because he was around people. Go be real. Go be connected with the people you work with instead of being a nonstop Superman. Go be Clark Kent, Jon."

She was right. Although I was getting better at finding ways to hone skills in my day job that would later serve me in my dream job, I'd never looked at it the other way.

I'd never taken the time to say, "How can this dream impact my job?" I had failed to see my job through the filter of my dream.

My dream that began with the Stuff Christians Like blog was about people. It was about creating honest conversations about a subject that sometimes doesn't get talked about in an honest way: faith. My purpose was to connect with people and create fresh dialogue about that part of my life. That's what the Stuff Christians Like blog and the book and ultimately that dream were all about.

Guess who I was surrounded by all day at work?

People.

In my ignorance, I had acted as if there were no way to use my dream to improve my day job. I was standing at a window, staring at the horizon, hoping, *Someday, my dream job will allow me to reach out to people and change lives. If only it would come sooner. I can't wait to connect with people!*

Then I would climb into my cubicle cave and ignore all my coworkers, who were people, by the way. Real people with real hopes and real dreams.

Seeing this gross oversight changed the way I looked at work. I had a higher purpose to go to all the meetings and fill out all the paperwork and work as hard as

I could on my projects. I still got grumpy and impatient at times, but more often than not I was able to remember my real purpose for being there. My dream-related purpose. People.

I don't know the details of your dream. I don't know how the purpose of your dream applies to your current job. But I know it involves people. On some level, every dream involves people. And unless your company is staffed by robots, save for you, you've already got the start of a purpose to change the way you look at work. And if you're honest about your dream job and honest about your day job, there's no end to the number of ways you can find greater meaning in one of the last places we tend to look— the place we spend at least forty hours a week.

Three pretty easy ways to ruin your day job and your dream job in the process

I'll admit it. Sometimes you haven't experienced a root canal in a long time, so working to avoid tooth agony is a really ineffective motivator. Sometimes you're single and you don't have kids or a wife or even an above-average cat you need to care for, so being able to support someone else isn't a highly motivating reason right now.

Some days, you'll be particularly eager to ignore all the reasons to fall in like with a job you don't love. Let's face it: Some days corporate sends out a memo that you can no longer have coffee at your desk and are now only allowed water and hard candy. Worse than that, they won't even explain what to do with caramel that starts off hard but goes chewy almost immediately. I literally had that day and many other more serious challenges that made surviving a day job feel impossible. Believe me, I get it.

When you write a book that has elements of your life in it, it's incredibly tempting to paint yourself as the hero. To shine your mistakes, overlook your stumbles and paint a smiley face over the experience.

I don't want to do that with the three years I spent at AutoTrader.com. In addition to many of those days being incredibly difficult, I also made a lot of mistakes along the way. In doing so, I discovered three pretty easy ways to ruin your day job and your dream job in the process. I hope the following missteps can serve as lessons you don't have to learn by personal experience.

One: Steal from work.

Don't ever complain about traffic around someone from Los Angeles. She will giggle, rub the top of your head, and tell you, "That's adorable." Then she will proceed to assert you have no idea what real traffic is. But regardless of what she might say, Atlanta traffic is legitimately gross. So while I lived there, I would "beat it" by leaving the house at 6 a.m. and doing personal writing at work before my workday started. If I wrote at home in the morning, I could almost hear Interstate 400 filling up and found it too distracting.

When the Stuff Christians Like blog first took off, I used to write each day's post about three minutes before it would go live, in my cubicle. Doing that meant there were some mornings when I wasn't quite finished by 8 a.m., when it was time to start doing my work for which I was being paid; 8:10 would come, then 8:20, and I was still blogging away. I was late for work even though I was physically there.

The romantic way to look at it is that my dream job bled over into my day job. The candid way to look at it is that I was stealing from work.

When you do your dream on work time, that's stealing from your employer. Look for the parallels between your day job and your dream job. Find a way to see how your dream's purpose can improve your job performance, but don't spend time doing something for which you are not being paid. Your employer didn't hire you to pursue your dream on work time. They hired you to fulfill a job description and you accepted it. You have a duty to complete that commitment.

It's tempting to ignore that commitment as your dream gains momentum. It was hard for me to work on a corporate memo when the chance to interact with thousands of people on my blog was calling me. This is my dream! So shiny! So fun! So not what I was hired to do.

The first lie we tell ourselves is that we'll just work longer hours and "make it up to them." But when you do that, work rarely wins. If someone is going to get cheated, it's usually not your dream.

The second lie we tell ourselves is that we're "able to get the forty-hour workload done in thirty-two hours" so, conveniently, we have eight hours left to work on our dream.

Efficiency is great. I love that you're killing it at work. But if you find more room in your day because you hustled, that's not your room. That's their room.

This was a struggle for me and I had to attack this monster in a number of different ways. The first is that I started to get ahead of my blog. I would write weeks in advance so that I never had the pressure of finishing something before work started. Scheduling my blog posts and tweets ahead of time helped me focus on work during the day.

The second thing I did was change the location I was pursuing my dream. I still preferred to write at work in order to avoid traffic, but now instead of my desk, I went to an empty conference room. In that room, in that hour, I could write whatever I wanted to. As soon as I left that room, though, it was business time. That small but surprisingly helpful physical separation created a good barrier for me between my dream job and my day job.

The third thing I did was find more work to do at AutoTrader.com. When I realized I was able to get all of my work done in less than forty hours, I actively filled that extra time with other AutoTrader.com related activities. I applied for two leadership programs. I got accepted to one and was able to continue working hard for the money they were paying me.

The final thing I did was treat AutoTrader.com like a client instead of a job. As a freelance writer, I would have never dreamed of billing a freelance client for hours I spent working on my dream. I only billed them for hours I spent working on their project. But in the average full-time job, especially at a medium-to-large company that isn't tracking billable hours, it's easy to forget that. It's all just one big pool of money and one big pool of working hours. You lose sight of the fact that real money and real consequences are involved with your actions. But if you flipped the circumstances around you'd never think it was right.

If you took your car to a mechanic and they charged you for seven hours of labor to fix it, you'd have a problem if three of those hours were spent spinning pottery. You'd be incredulous if when you complained about the bill they said, "We're sorry. Pottery is our mechanic's dream. He loved *Ghost*. We put a wheel and kiln behind our shop and he just really got into it the other day. He made some beautiful vases."

Even though I was an office employee and not paid hourly like a mechanic, I began treating AutoTrader.com like a client. And it helped. Not only did I stop stealing time from work because they purchased forty hours of work, not just forty hours of my presence; I also began protecting my dream better.

I was more than happy to work the occasional overtime that certain projects required. But I never had to make a habit of it—and face stealing time from my dream job—because I was honest and diligent with my day job hours.

Two: Think of your job as your
adversary, not your advocate.

When I worked at AutoTrader.com, I thought I got pretty good at seeing the company as a patron of my dream. When I got to use a vacation day to go speak at a conference, I recognized, "Wow, I'm getting paid by AutoTrader.com to be here today. They are helping to pay for my dream." I thought I was doing a great job of seeing them as an advocate and not my adversary, until I got my dream job.

Six months into working at Dave Ramsey, my team leader set an aggressive goal to sell a lot of copies of this book. The goal felt really daunting and scary to me when I thought about it. My first thought was, *I'll never make this goal happen.* That changed to, *I'm going to fail at this goal.* And finally I landed on, *He wants me to fail!* I started to see my team leader as an adversary, not a supporter. I started to get worried that my dream was getting attacked by that sales goal. It wasn't. Not even a little. My team leader actually wanted my dream to succeed more than I did. Here's a text message he sent me one night: "I feel a great responsibility to make sure you succeed. (As defined by the greatest number of people hearing your message through multiple mediums.) Thanks for trusting us with your gifts."

Does that sound like an adversary or an opponent of my dream? Of course not, so why did I feel differently?

I had just spent twelve years of my professional career feeling at odds with the companies I worked at. I spent a dozen years thinking I needed to scrap and fight for my dream against "the man." It was me against the world! For over a decade I looked at my job with an adversary mentality. When I finally reached my dream job, I had a really hard time not defaulting to that line of thinking.

It's a way of thinking that first takes seed when you have to work a job that might not be perfectly lined up with your dream. Wage war against this poisonous thought. Do everything in your power to protect the way you look at your boss and your company. To the best of your abilities and reality, see them as patrons, advocates and supporters, not enemies. It will make your time there easier and give you a much better shot at success when you close the gap between your day job and your dream job.

Three: Demand that your job meet the needs of your dream.

Nothing kills a day job and a dream job faster than feeling like you're entitled to both. I scowled my way through dozens of meetings at AutoTrader.com with a heart full of ungratefulness. At Bose, I almost got fired and was called "aloof" (a major insult for someone whose gift is motivation), because I was so mad at that environment. On top of that I added a degree of arrogance to my jambalaya of funk once my dream got a little successful.

When my blog got big, I tried to help AutoTrader.com with social media. I had personally learned a lot about the wild, wild West that was social media and thought I might have something to offer. But that wasn't my position. I wasn't in marketing. I wasn't in product development. I was in IT. So despite my best attempts to contribute ideas about blogging, they really didn't need me to.

At first this killed me. On the outside of the building I was speaking around the country on social media and growing one of the largest Christian blogs on the planet. But on the inside of the company I wasn't doing anything remotely related to blogging. I remember one meeting where we brought in an expensive outside expert to teach us all about blogging. I made a point in the middle of the meeting and she proceeded to tear me apart, saying something like, "You're wrong about blogging. You don't know about blogging or social media. You should learn about it."

I called my wife as I walked back to my building after the meeting and told her that I appreciated the opportunity to learn humility. Or I told her I hated my job and was terribly disappointed that my stupid dream wouldn't happen already. It was one of the two.

Instead of looking for parallels between my day job and my dream job, I started to demand them. I started to feel entitled to them, as though I deserved them. I didn't, though. My job had no obligation to meet all my dreams. They'd been clear about that all along. They hadn't changed. Only my attitude had.

I hope there are countless overlaps between your day job and your dream job. I hope it's incredibly easy to see the parallels and find a purpose there, but sometimes it won't be. And when it's not, don't demand that your job meet the needs of your dream. That's not what your job is for.

Besides, that's not our ultimate goal anyway. I only want you to fall in like with a job you don't love. You've already got one true love, your dream. And it's time to do something about that.

CHAPTER 5

Wait on the Main Stage

"We've got to get you on the main stage."

My friend said this when I told him that a leadership group named Catalyst asked me to speak at all three of their events in 2011. Just not on the main stage.

Catalyst is one of the largest leadership conferences in the country and is broken up into primarily two sections, main stage and labs. The conference is officially a two-day event, starting on Thursday and finishing on Friday. More than 13,000 people attend. On Wednesday, as a kind of pregame, they hold small lab sessions. About 4,000 people attend these and there are usually close to 100 different sessions you can choose from.

So the difference of being on the main stage versus a lab is significant. On the main stage you speak at the Gwinnett Center to more than 13,000 people on a stage built of LED lights that is U2-worthy. In the lab, you speak to at best a few hundred people in a conference room in an adjacent building that may have held a luncheon for Atlanta tax attorneys the day before.

The main stage is an admirable goal and having spoken at three labs in the past two years, it is one a few of my friends have wanted me to have achieved already. Meant as a compliment, as a "Go get 'em, tiger, you're good enough to speak on the main stage!" those words often get a little twisted in my head. What I hear when people ask me about the main stage is, "What's wrong with you? Why haven't they asked you to speak on the main stage yet? Speaking at a lab is a failure. Didn't you already speak at a bunch of labs? If you're not careful you're going to get stuck at 'lab level' and they'll never see you as a main-stage guy."

Although you might not have the ability to turn a positive question from a friend into a paragraph-long denouncement of your dream, you have experienced moments when you didn't feel like things were progressing fast enough. You've tasted a bit of the dream and thought, *This is it! It's go time! I'm throwing caution to the wind!*

I completely agree with you.

This is the march to the main stage! We need to get going! There are tons of really amazing things to do!

But I want us to go slow.

I want us to go small.

I want us to get comfortable with being "lab level."

Why?

Because it's the only real way to reach *and* stay on the main stage. And it starts with a plan.

The Plan Myth

You would start today if you had a good plan. You would begin radically changing your life and quite possibly the lives of everyone around you, if you only had a decent plan in front of you.

Don't get me wrong. Plans are important. For everything from budgets to getting a business off the ground, a plan is a necessary part of any endeavor. But something weird happens when we use them as an excuse not to get started on our dream.

When we think of obstacles that stand between us and how we want to live, we rarely would accuse our desire to have a plan as being one of them. A plan is always presented as a smart, logical step in whatever you want to do. Plans are mature. They are wise. They are critical. But like a lot of other good things in life, they can get corrupted. And if we look at them the wrong way, we start to believe the Plan Myth.

The Plan Myth is a tiny voice that pipes up whenever we bump into people who are doing the things we would like to do. When confronted with someone else who is in the field or industry or dream we want for our own lives, we automatically assume that we are looking at the fruition of a long, detailed plan. We believe that years ago, on a blank wall like in the movie *Ocean's Eleven*, this person mapped out his entire life first.

That individual had the vision and the dream to actually plan out what was going to happen, and now it is. Now it has come to pass. He did it with a plan, and we need one too.

Until it's in place there's really no point in getting started. We need to plan first and then act. We need to be meticulous and detailed in the way we architect the next month or year or decade. We will "plan the work and then work the plan."

We will read a book that has steps on the cover. We will attend a conference that promises a bulletproof business plan and immediate success. We will search "career" on Amazon, see there are 115,656 books, and buy the three we think will most quickly deliver us a perfect plan.

But then, awash in the fire-hose spray that is the Plan Myth, we stop. It's overwhelming and we quit. We will give up before we've even really started. Why?

Because plans are challenging and it's difficult to try to reduce to steps the actions that take us from ordinary right now to extraordinary later. Where do you even start? Furthermore, in what format should the plan be? Should it be large and graphic, sprawling across our walls at home, or detailed and quiet, confined to an Excel spreadsheet?

So we freeze. We pause and we get stuck. But here's a secret, something I found a little surprising. The most successful people in the world often didn't start with a detailed plan.

The most dramatic stories, the inspirations that move our hearts and our minds, are not born from people who mechanically followed the orchestrated steps of a plan. All too often, the stories that grip us are the lives where someone lived with passion long before they lived with a plan.

Malcolm Gladwell, the best-selling author of books like *Blink* and *The Tipping Point*, discussed this one time. In a speech he admitted, "I didn't plan or predict the success of *Tipping Point*."[11] It took him a long time to get to that point. We might see the success and think Gladwell just laid out the steps carefully and then executed them, but he didn't. If that had been the case, he would have planned that success a long time ago. Why wait until you're in your thirties or forties? Why not just become hugely successful right away? If plans guaranteed success, we would all plan to have it much earlier in life.

A soccer player would never say, "I scored that goal because I had a detailed plan." He wouldn't say, "You know how that corner kick came at me in that arch and the defender timed his jump too early, and a late spring breeze made the ball rise at the last second and the sun made the goalie lose it because of where he was standing? I planned that. That's why I was able to bounce it off the perfect part of my head into the only unreachable corner of the net."

No one would say that. No one could.

So why then do we buy the Plan Myth when it comes to other areas of life? How can we possibly believe that there are too many variables in a soccer goal but not so in life? Surely the average day carries more variables than the average soccer game. There are only twenty-two players on a soccer field. You might interact with hundreds of people today. Each one of those people adds an element of the unexpected to your day. Plan all you want but you'll never be able to script every detail.

That's not to say plans can't be great. They can. That soccer player planned his training. He planned his field position. He planned what type of strike he would make if the ball happened his way. He planned a lot of different things, but the plans didn't prevent him from acting; they gave him direction in acting.

Don't let the Plan Myth paralyze you. A plan is not the first thing you need. Often, it is the third.

The first thing you need is a passion. Like Malcolm Gladwell's unquenchable curiosity to explore the unexpected relationships between things, you need a passion that will drive you forward. You need a love, a hope, a dream that is yours. That is the first thing you need, your WHY, as Simon Sinek suggests. The thing you've recovered.

The second thing you need is practice. You need to try what you're interested in. You need to dip your foot in the water. You need to visit stores like the one you want to open. You need to read blogs like the one you want to start. You need to explore and test the waters. When asked about the secret of his success, Warren Buffett, the third-richest man on the planet said, "There's no place where we turned the switch. So much happens by accident. It does show the value of showing up every day."

After you've identified your dream and made a habit of showing up every day, then you can start detailing your plan. Once you've got a little taste for what you want to do, a detailed plan can work miracles. Once you've got at least a sense of where you're headed, a plan can be incredibly invaluable.

When I started Stuff Christians Like in March 2008 in Atlanta, I didn't have a plan that in January 2011 I'd be a full-time author with the Dave Ramsey team, living in Nashville. I didn't write the word *Nashville* on a whiteboard and draw out my plan to get there. I had a passion to write, so I came up with a rough plan to do that. I had a loose plan that involved me writing on the internet on a regular basis. That's it. Then I practiced doing that on the blog for months and months. Hinge moments came, reshaping my passion and adding important details to my plan. Over time I learned to plan out posts weeks in advance and set some goals I planned to hit. I stayed flexible to allow the plan to develop as I continued to practice.

I once heard innolution.com's Kenny Rubin ask, "Why do we make our most important plans and decisions at the point in the project when we have the least amount of information?" His point was that we are at our most ignorant about what the future holds in a project on the first day. We don't know what obstacles or opportunities lie ahead. We often have the least amount of intel on what might happen. Still we tend to lock ourselves into elaborate plans and then suffer the consequences later when circumstances refuse to cooperate. He illustrated his point by telling a story about his friend, an extreme skier.

Rubin asked this friend if he planned his entire run from the top of the mountain. The friend told him he didn't. He planned about four moves out at a time. By the time he made it to his fourth move, he could see the terrain differently. There'd be a rock face he couldn't see from the top or the light would have changed and he could see ice in a different way now. The conditions radically changed by the time he got to the fourth move, so his plan did too.

The conditions of your dream will change as quickly as that mountain face. New opportunities will come into view. Unexpected obstacles will arise. And while your passion will remain the same, your plan has to be flexible enough to accommodate them. This isn't just true of sarcastic blogs and extreme skiers. This principle works for people who want to build multimillion-dollar businesses too.

When the leader of the company I work for, Dave Ramsey, started EntreLeadership, he followed the Passion, Practice, Plan model I just described.

As Dave's core business grew, he was extremely intentional about opening up his leadership playbook to his central group of leaders. He was passionate about pouring that experience into them. Once things really started moving in the company, other team members started asking questions about the whys of how Dave led the business. So, he started teaching the whole team these "EntreLeadership" (part entrepreneur, part leadership) principles.

In one of the weekly training sessions, Dave looked up and noticed that he didn't recognize half the people in the room. His team members were bringing their friends, spouses, pastors and neighbors to hear this material. He recalls thinking, *I'm no genius, but I think there may be a business in this material.*

That was the hinge moment when EntreLeadership became something else. What started as a way to train his own team grew into a way to train other leaders. Now, Dave has put thousands of business leaders from across the country through his live training, and he even wrote a book based on these principles.

He had a passion.

Then he practiced it.

Then he planned it.

Focus on your passion first. Your passion will always fuel your plan. Rarely will a plan fuel a passion. It will contribute. It will shape it. It will most certainly help it. But the biggest leaders, the most successful people, will tell you a passion for something drove them long before a plan did.

David didn't know Cinderella

We love a good underdog story.

We love watching someone much smaller and weaker defeat a much larger and stronger opponent. Great examples occur every spring as part of March Madness. The NCAA Men's Basketball Tournament amplifies the drama by ranking each team and pitting the strongest against the weakest. The number-one seed plays the number-sixteen seed. The number-two seed plays the number-fifteen seed, and so forth. The eight-versus-nine game is nowhere near as captivating as the potential of an upset between a number one and a number sixteen. Those are our favorite games, and we turn out in droves to see if the Richmond Spiders can beat a powerhouse like Syracuse.

We love these stories in part because we all want to be David. Regardless of your belief system, you can't watch sports and not hear this story referenced.

David, a shepherd so small and insignificant he couldn't even fit in a set of adult armor, defeats a ten-foot-tall giant with a single stone and swings the entire future of a nation. It is a powerful story that connects on a lot of levels with people of all ages, but we've heard it so many times that we've probably missed some critical elements of it.

We miss them because we get that story all tangled up with the Cinderella story. Both stories are often trotted out by sportscasters. In the same sentence, they will say, "This game is a classic David versus Goliath. Samford University is a real Cinderella story." The two stories get wrapped up together into one homogenized underdog metaphor.

Long shot goes up against impossible odds and somehow wins. Beautiful story. The end.

It makes for a great story, but when applied to real life, our desire for an underdog story quickly falls apart. There are a number of ways the David and Goliath story is very different from Cinderella and they impact the way your dream is probably going to unfold.

The hinge moment for Cinderella, a story of a young woman who falls in love with a prince and escapes her evil stepmother, is the ball. Wearing clothes given to her by her fairy godmother, Cinderella attends the king's gala event and dances with the prince. They fall in love but she must leave by midnight. He is left holding a single glass slipper and a heart full of questions. Ahhh. The next day one of the king's men comes to Cinderella's house in search of the mysterious girl. He slips on the glass slipper, they realize it is her, she marries the prince, and they live happily ever after. Kisses. Hugs. The first step toward running the eventual Disney princess cartel is in place. The end.

It's a sweet story, but it's also incredibly quick and easy. Cinderella may have spent years laboring under an evil stepmother, but after her hinge moment, things happen for her almost instantly.

This is not David's story, which is a better frame of reference for the path you should expect when chasing your dream job.

David might not have had an evil stepmother like Cinderella, but his dad, Jesse, showed him about as much love. When a prophet came to find the new king from among the sons of Jesse, David's father didn't even invite him in from the fields. Cinderella wasn't invited to the king's ball, and David wasn't invited to be king.

But the similarities between the two stories start to break down there. Like Cinderella, David was deemed royalty soon thereafter. But unlike Cinderella, David did not take his place for a long time.

When the prophet Samuel couldn't find a king among David's many brothers, he asked Jesse if there was another son. David was soon anointed to become the king of Israel. It was a powerful moment. It was a life-changing moment. And then David returned to shepherding. For several years.

Hold up. Cinderella didn't sweat for years after her glass slipper moment. She was a princess in a matter of days.

David was back to being a shepherd the next day. Maybe the same day. How long can it take to pour some oil on a kid's head?

Regardless of being anointed as the king, he immediately returned to the solitary life of sheep and big skies and big dreams, with oil on his head but a simple staff in his hand. It would be years before he'd ascend to the throne. He didn't hit main stage right away.

Cinderella's hinge moment is about as dramatic as you get. In the Disney version, it starts with a group of adorable animals making her a dress. Mice literally band together to do a kind of *Project Runway* moment for her, but her stepsisters ruin it. They rip her dress up and mock her for thinking she could go to the ball.

Into that moment steps a fairy godmother. She turns a pumpkin into a carriage, gives Cinderella a magical dress, and saves the day. The moment is glittery and loud like a Mariah Carey video. Cinderella goes to the ball, instantly wins over the prince, and they fall in love. Big drama. Big fireworks. Big finish.

And that's how we want our dreams to go down. We don't just want Catalyst to call us and offer us a chance to speak at a lab to forty-five people. We want an invite to speak on the main stage to 13,000. We don't want a local store to order ten of the crafts we make. We want Walmart to call and order 10,000. We want Cinderella. We tend to get David.

His story continues with Israel fighting a battle against the Philistines. The entire nation of Israel was terrified. A giant named Goliath taunted them from across enemy lines. When David arrived on the scene, his brothers mocked him. In a very stepsister moment, they tore him down and berated him for being there.

That was David's big moment, another hinge moment, his version of the ball. Surely he was there for some dramatic reason. Surely his journey to that moment had started with something miraculous happening, like a pumpkin carriage and a bunch of singing, sewing sheep.

But do you know why David was there that day? Do you know what he was doing when he encountered Goliath?

He was delivering lunch to his brothers. The anointed king, the boy with God's hand on him, the future leader of Israel, was delivering sandwiches.

I don't technically know if they were sandwiches. They were probably falafels, but that's beside the point.

He wasn't attending a royal ball in a magical carriage, wearing curiously comfortable glass slippers. He didn't experience a wave of pomp and circumstance that propelled him into a magical moment. He brought lunch, something that was common for the youngest brother who was too young to do the "real" work on the front lines.

I like that because so often developing our dream job is less about grand balls at grand castles and more about bringing lunch. It's a process of doing small but necessary things, over and over again, and letting the momentum build, instead of getting decked out by a fairy godmother and being escorted to prominence in a blinged-out carriage.

I want to speak on the Catalyst main stage. I want to speak on platforms even bigger than that. But I know I need to do a lot of little things before I stand before Goliath. I want quiet-big moments long before I have loud-big moments. I want to have two people show up to one of my events and deal with the awkwardness of that before I try to lasso the moon.

Not because I'm humble, something I have rarely been accused of. I just want to get great before I step onto a Goliath-sized playing field. I don't want to wow 100 people in an audience of 13,000. I want to reach all 13,000. You should too.

Right now, the size of your dream probably outweighs your ability by at least tenfold. That's not a bad thing. I love that you've got a big dream right now. I love that you've got your own personal version of the Catalyst main stage. I think that's important, I just don't want you to get lost chasing a Cinderella story when what leads to a true happily-ever-after experience is a David story.

Start small. Start slow. Get better along the way. And enjoy the gift of making many of your early mistakes without a major audience.

Enjoy the gift of invisibility

Seth Godin clarifies this idea in his book *The Dip* when he quotes Sergey Brin, the founder of Google, about their early strategy.

"We knew that Google was going to get better every single day as we worked on it, and we knew that sooner or later, everyone was going to try it. So our feeling was that the later you tried it, the better it was for us because we'd make a better impression with better technology. So we were never in a big hurry to get you to use it today. Tomorrow would be better."[12]

There are many circumstances for which waiting is much more favorable than Cinderella success. Developing your dream job is one of them.

For about a year before I started StuffChristiansLike.net, I wrote a blog called Prodigal Jon. On my best day, 200 people showed up and read what I wrote. On the average day, fifty people did. And a lot of those fifty people had the same last name I did. And were my mom.

It was a quiet blog that by blogging terms wasn't very successful. If the goal of a blog is to grow an active, vocal community, then I was failing. Almost no one read it, and even though I worked as hard as I could, it stayed roughly the same size. Day after day, month after month, I wrote Prodigal Jon.

At the time, I felt like it wasn't going anywhere. I felt confused that so few people knew about it. I didn't see the point of writing to a handful of people on a consistent basis.

That didn't make a whole lot of sense to me. But looking back on it, I needed that year. I needed the gift so few of us want but most of us need: the gift of invisibility.

When you start something new, you want it to be successful right away. You want it to grow and get visible quickly. But there are some problems inherent to visibility.

For starters, it's harder to take risks when people are watching you. It's harder to experiment when many eyeballs are tracking with you. It's harder to remain innovative when people have a specific expectation about who you are and what you do.

The temptation to play it safe increases with each new fan or follower. Suddenly, instead of just doing what you love to do, other people are speaking into it with their hopes and plans. People tend to get safe and small in the spotlight.

Your honesty also seems inversely proportionate to the size of your audience. Your willingness to be open shrinks in proportion to the growth of your crowd. It's not that difficult to be transparent to a group of ten readers. You realize that if you say something they don't like and they all stop supporting your dream, you can always start over.

But if you've got 4,000 people buying your product or using the services of your company, you now have 4,000 reasons to keep things polished and pretty.

Let's think about this whole honesty thing. It's the reverse of every Jerry Bruckheimer "guy goes on a revenge streak" movie. The tagline for those is usually something like, "The most dangerous man in the world is the man who has nothing to lose." The opposite of that, especially if you get some attention and visibility for your dream early on, is, "The safest man in the world is the man who has everything to lose."

It's true. One of the costs of notoriety is safety.

Anonymity allows you to make big, gross mistakes without everyone watching. Anonymity is the best creative lab because you've got nothing to lose. Anything is possible. Anything is on the table. There are no expectations to miss, no fans to disappoint, no follow-up fears.

That's why famous writers are so terrified to follow up on success. I've heard mega best-selling authors confess that when they sat down to try to write their next book they were overwhelmed with fear. The expectations, the hope that they would re-create the success of that first book, that they would catch lightning in a bottle again, were so high that they almost crippled them.

You don't have that issue if you are invisible and anonymous.

You're free. As long as you are invisible, you have what Justin Bieber and Martha Stewart and LeBron James will never have again—the freedom to make mistakes on your own.

That might not seem like much. That might seem more like a punishment than a gift sometimes, but it's true. Being out of the public eye is the perfect opportunity for you to get better at what you do before you go really big.

I know that, culturally speaking, we often refuse to see invisibility as a gift. The sad thing is that you often don't learn that until it's too late. Eminem knows this.

I read an article in a magazine about his return to the top from a battle with drug addiction. The article mentioned that one of the things he likes to do is drive back to the small house he grew up in, sit slouched in his car so people can't tell it's him, and reminisce about a time when life was simpler. He says, "It may sound corny, but I'll go by and try to remember how things were when we were in those houses. As time goes by, you might get content and forget things." He's concerned about losing that part of his life, that drive, now that he's no longer invisible and connected to the same hunger.[13]

You might never be Eminem, but someday, I promise you, you will treasure and value this time when your dream job was just a dream. A time when you were invisible and able to make big mistakes without big embarrassment. A time when things were simple and the canvas wasn't surrounded by thousands, even millions, of onlookers awaiting every brush stroke.

I think you're going to do great things. I think you probably already have and having visibility is going to give you so many opportunities invisibility never could. But don't see invisibility as a punishment or a failure. See it as a gift. See it as something fleeting that is worth cherishing while it's still around. Don't rush through the one chapter that celebrities like Eminem long to stay connected to.

Stay dangerous. Stay bold. And for longer than you probably want to, stay invisible.

Get comfortable in Nebraska

My friend Rachel is just starting to chase her dream job. She wants to travel the country, speaking about finances to her generation of high school and college students. Her dad is Dave Ramsey, and he's built an incredibly large platform doing the same for millions of people through his radio program. Rachel grew up watching him and learning the ropes. Now, at the age of 22, she's starting to get her own opportunities to speak to her own audience, and fortunately it's going slowly.

I talked to her about that one day. A van full of us were riding back from a sold-out event in Orlando that her dad had done in front of 9,000 people. It was a beautiful fall day there and the energy of the experience was electric. And twenty-four hours later, Rachel would be in Nebraska.

In the middle of November she would be flying to rural Nebraska to speak to thirty people. And when we face moments like that, it's easy to get discouraged.

Nobody comes to your event. Nobody donates to your charity. Nobody reads your blog. You can run a ten-million-dollar project at work, but when it comes to your dream job, you can't even get the freelance designer to finish your website.

That's a tough pill to swallow. But like I told Rachel as she left the safety and size of her dad's platform, that's okay. These are the Nebraska years.

These are the years when you'll travel 2,000 miles in cold temperatures to speak to fewer people than an NFL team. These are the years you'll throw away canvas after canvas because the colors refuse to cooperate. These are the years you'll teach three people how to swing dance when the studio space you rented would fit eighty.

These are the Nebraska years and the sooner you quit being surprised by the hardship of them, the sooner you can survive. Not just survive, but actually thrive. With a Rocky-climbing-the-stairs enthusiasm you can eventually start to see the odds stacked against you as exhilarating.

That's how I felt when I wrote my first book. The blog I started with was based on another blog. My blog wasn't an original idea, and lots of people pointed this out to me. Leaders and well-respected industry in-siders would say, "That's just the kid who ripped off the Stuff White People Like blog." And at first I was hurt by that, in part because I wanted it to be easy. I didn't want to go to Nebraska. I wanted to leave the safety of my blog and find the exact same support as I stepped out to write a book.

I didn't. I had events where two people showed up. I've watched hundreds of people pick up my book while I was standing at a signing table, shrug and then walk away without saying a word to me. I've flown 3,000 miles to speak to twenty people only to have some of them walk out in the first three minutes of my speech.

But these are the Nebraska years. This is the gift of invisibility. This is what it means to start out small and remain patient.

And the truth is that a few people is all you need to keep going. Those thirty people in Nebraska or the two people in the pottery workshop you put on in Cleveland matter. Infinitely so.

When you first start out, expect the Nebraska years. Every dream goes through Nebraska.

But we're not going to stay there. I promise. We're going to grow our dream bigger than the cornfields. We're going to take it to new places and new heights.

And we're going to get there because we hustle.

CHAPTER 6

There Will Be Hustle

"It must be awesome to have a full-time job like Stuff Christians Like. I would love that."

That's something I heard for two years as I traveled around the country speaking at conferences or churches. The perception was that my job was simply to write a blog that referenced the Kardashians and the Old Testament in the same sentence, and then speak from time to time at fun places. I wish.

Technically speaking, I've never taken my blogging full time and especially not then. At the time people thought I was a professional blogger, I was working in an IT department. I was using vacation days to go to conferences. Toward the end of each year I would have to say no to almost everyone who asked me to speak because I ran out of days and couldn't steal from the Thanksgiving or Christmas jar.

I'd do radio interviews from the car during lunch and schedule tweets so that I could try to avoid stealing time from work. I carved up my day into a million pieces trying to fit a dream job around a day job. And it ultimately worked because I hustled.

That's a funny word to me. When we started thinking about titling this book, one of the ideas we had was to call it *Hustle*. The name did pretty well in our brainstorming room until someone said, "That sounds too much like streetwalking or prostitution." Having long ago promised both my parents that I would never write a book about hookers, I relented. We changed the title.

I love the title *Quitter* but still think that a core element holding this entire book together is a need to hustle. To push harder than the other person. To dream further. To work longer and faster and this is starting to sound a little like a Kanye West/Daft Punk remix.

Put it this way: I don't think any of the information in this book works without applying hustle to it. That's the key. To this book and maybe even to your dream.

The simple truth about hustle

I am related to Roy Acuff. If that means something to you, then congratulations, you've been to the Grand Ole Opry in Nashville and may or may not own a fiddle. Owning a fiddle or at least an ear for fiddlin' greatly increases the odds of your hearing my last name and saying, "Acuff? Any kin to Roy?" He's known as "the King of Country Music" and has a theater named after him at the Grand Ole Opry. When people ask me if we're related, I have one joke that I always do and it's not that funny so I'm not sure why I keep doing it. I always say, "We're related, but not so close that I don't have to work!" Then we laugh a little and I inevitably say, "He's my third or fourth cousin. It's not like I've got bluegrass money."

I think that joke might have been C, maybe C-plus quality the first time I used it, but it has significantly deteriorated each day I've lived in Tennessee. People keep asking me about my cousin Roy. But I wish they were asking me about my cousin Charlie.

Charlie isn't really my cousin. He married my wife's cousin, which makes him one of those relatives with whom you never bother to figure out the calculus-like equation of how you're related. But Charlie is easily my favorite cousin, and I promise, you have one too. This is the relative you always try to sit next to at family gatherings. This is the relative whose very presence increases the likelihood of your attending events. "Is Charlie going to be there?" is a question my wife is tired of hearing me ask. Why do I like Charlie so much?

He tells the best stories. He's thirty years old, from low-country South Carolina and quintessentially Southern. He's also a firefighter at two different stations, which gives him plenty of fodder for what I guess you would call "yarns." So when I find him at family events, he is quick to tell me things like: "I got called out to a scene down a dark highway one night. Some guy had hit a deer. Just wrecked his car, deer is layin' spread out on the side of the road.

All of the sudden, a pickup truck pulls up alongside of me and rolls the window down. Guy leans out and says, 'You gonna keep that deer?'"

At this point, having very little experience with carcass negotiations, I am fascinated. "What did you do?" I asked Charlie.

"I helped him load the deer into the back of his truck and he drove off."

If you eat Thanksgiving with Charlie, you are guaranteed at least seven stories exactly like this. That's what I've come to know and love about Charlie. But one Christmas he caught me off guard.

My wife's extended family had planned a big ski trip to Crested Butte. A friend had donated a massive 10,000-square-foot house for all us to stay in for the week. But ski ticket prices and flights to Colorado were still expensive. I asked Charlie if he and his wife were going to be able to make it.

"Well, I'm working double shifts and overtime at both stations. It's not easy, because Hillary wants me home more, but every time I leave the house, I ask her, 'Do you really want to go to Colorado?' If she says 'Yes,' then I say, 'I'll see you tomorrow,' and then I go to work."

Hustle is really that simple.

We often try to make it complicated. We say things like, "I don't even know where to start" or "I just don't have the time" or, "I'm afraid to do it the wrong way," when it comes to hard work and putting in effort. But our desire to complicate it is all too often just a cover for laziness or fear.

If you wait until night to work on your dream, you will often spend the whole day gathering up material for excuses on why you shouldn't do what it is you feel called to do.

"I need to clean up."

"I have to return a few phone calls."

"I just need to unwind."

Your day rolls toward night like an excuse snowball barreling down a hill, packing on more excuses with every rotation.

Do you know when you have a lot fewer excuses to claw your way through? In the morning. Nobody wakes up and wants to balance their checkbook. Few can return phone calls at 5 a.m. There's nothing good on TV, and watching shows you've TiVo'd before the crack of dawn feels a little weird. The only excuse you have to deal with is being tired, but that's one you can work through over time. Or forget working through it over time. Go to bed earlier. See that? I just eliminated the excuse. You're welcome.

If it's not an excuse that keeps you from working on your dream in the evening, it will be another competitive option that distracts you. The guy you've been dying to go out with calls you unexpectedly and asks you to dinner. A friend you haven't seen for weeks pops in. You have to work late because a project blew up at the office.

Again, do you know when those things are not happening? In the morning.

If a guy asks you to breakfast at 5 a.m., don't date him. That is a stupid time for a date, even if it involves a hot air balloon like the one that emergency landed in my driveway one morning. That girl didn't look so happy. And someone who pops in at 5 a.m. isn't popping in. They are breaking in. Last but not least, a project you are working on at your job is very unlikely to need you at 5 a.m. Bosses come in all the time at 5 p.m. for things they need done right away. But I've never had a boss knock on my bedroom door before the sun comes up and say, "Acuff, I need you to work on this. It's critical. So critical I'm standing in your bedroom at 5 a.m."

That just doesn't happen often.

For me, excuses aren't the only thing I have less of in the morning. My doubt tends to sleep in. My self-esteem gets up before the sun. I don't know if the "who are you to do that?" beast sleeps late too, but I certainly feel capable of more in the morning.

In addition to my blog, I also wrote the book *Stuff Christians Like* every morning before work because I felt as though my reserve of energy, creativity and curiosity got chipped away all day. When you're falling in like with a job you don't love, you will work hard at your company. You will often be empty by the time you get home from work, with nothing left for your dream.

The unexpected benefit is that if you work on your dream in the morning, it gives you a natural boost that can last the entire day. There's a great sense of joy that comes from accomplishing something that moves you closer to your dream job. There's a sense that regardless of what the day brings, you started with the work you love. You started by doing what matters to you most. That sense of joy and contentment can make the rest of your day even better.

When I was "full" after a morning of writing my own stuff, I was much less likely to demand that AutoTrader. com fulfill that role. By hustling in the morning for thirty minutes to an hour and a half, I could do my day job with a much better perspective.

Even if you're a night owl, I'm not sure the same can be said of working on your dream strictly at night. Sleeping tends to reset that good feeling. You might fall asleep with a sense of accomplishment, but it usually won't carry into the next day or fuel you as you work your day job. In fact, you'll likely fall prey to what we like to call "short-timer's disease." You might stay focused on your day job tasks until lunch, but once that clock strikes one you will be counting down the minutes to the time you can get back to your dream job.

The like versus love list

None of my friends will admit to watching an entire episode of *Jersey Shore*. (If you're reading this from the future, and this intimate look at life in New Jersey is off the air, imagine the book *Lord of the Flies*, powered by Red Bull and Axe body spray.)

If you ask my friends if they have seen the show, they will respond, "I caught a little while flipping channels."

Somewhere, millions of people are watching whole episodes, but apparently I don't know any of those people. Or all my friends are liars. It's one of those two.

The grandfather of *Jersey Shore* was a show called *The Real World*. It was a similar concept: throw attractive, opinionated people in a house they couldn't normally afford. Add liquor. Shake.

To be honest, I used to watch not only whole episodes of that show, I'd watch marathons. I'd sit down and not blink for hours without realizing it. Time, space, common sense, all forms of normal life were put on hold when I'd watch *The Real World*. But when I got married, that changed.

It changed because you start to realize the silliness of giving a show like that four hours of your life, especially when you say it out loud. "Oh, you wanted to go out to that café for brunch with some friends? That's one thing we could do. Or we could watch two hundred and forty straight minutes of MTV's *The Real World*."

That kind of thing happens a lot when you get married. It's not "your" time anymore; it's "our" time. A layer of selfishness gets worn away, which might feel more like torn away as you start sharing your time with someone other than yourself.

Then you have kids and your time gets even smaller. You go from "your time" to "our time" to "their time." An additional layer of selfishness gets stripped and you find yourself with a very different clock than you had when you were young and single and watching someone intoxicated debate the merits of jumping off a roof into a pool on *The Real World Cancun.*

The misconception is that you have less time to do the things you love when you get really busy. And it's a misconception that will carry over into your pursuit of trying to balance a full-time dream and a full-time job.

The reality is that when you get busy doing the things that matter to you, you actually have more time to do the things you love and less time to do the things you like.

Working on your dream job and your day job forces you to decide which things are a priority to you.

It forces you to make a like vs. love list.

Because you won't have as much time for the things you like. Just like I couldn't spend four hours watching *The Real World* marathons once I got married and had kids. I liked doing that, but I didn't love doing that. If I had a free hour, I wanted to invest it wisely. I wanted to spend it jogging or writing or doing something that mattered to me. My hours cost me too much to spend them on *The Real World.* If my wife and kids were out of town, I planned my time accordingly so I could get some freelance work done and hustle on the *Stuff Christians Like* book. I gave up some freedom for doing things I liked, but what I gained was a tremendous amount of love.

Though on the surface I was busy, I was actually spending a ton of time on things I loved. More so than I ever did when I was single and not making decisions based on my list.

That's one of the simple rules of hustle. Do more of the things you love and less of the things you like. Make your hustle matter. That's not to demonize TV or any other activity people might classify as downtime. But be deliberate about what is really a like and what is really a love. And then hustle to keep love a bigger part of your day than like.

The unfortunate relationship between quantity and quality

I've become the kind of author I used to hate. I'm not talking about the guy with elbow patches on his corduroy jacket and a pipe in his mouth and a wry barb about the Spanish-American war. I've got no problem with that guy. In the right setting I find him delightful. The person I really used to dislike is the author who told me writing was hard work and took time.

I wanted writing a book to be easy and simple and above all fast. So when I'd read books on writing and they'd say, "Write 500 words every day for a year," or, "Write and rewrite and rewrite some more," I'd feel like my dream had done the old bait-and-switch on me.

I thought chasing my dream would be easy. If you love something and feel passionate about it, shouldn't it on some level always come naturally? When I think of the stereotype of people who follow their dream, I think of someone glistening with syrupy happiness, not sweat. They laugh the day away and have tickle fights and long conversations with good friends under shade trees.

That was my impression of what it means to follow your dream. It might have been hard work, but it was work you loved so you didn't notice it was difficult or frustrating at times. It didn't "feel like work at all." It flowed out of you with very little effort.

I was wrong.

Chasing your dream is not like that.

Fulfilling your dream is not like that.

Closing the gap between a day job and a dream job is not really like that.

So I became the author I used to hate.

When people ask me, "How do you get a book published?" which is just a specific way to ask, "How do you make your dream happen?" they want the same answer I used to want.

"It's actually pretty easy. You just write a draft of a book, usually over a long weekend, in a cabin somewhere with a vista. Gotta have a vista. Then after you write it you give it to a publisher. They fall in love usually faster than it took you to write it. Then you go on a book tour that is highly attended and not at all just you sitting by an empty table watching people pick up your life's work, flip through it, shrug in disappointment, and walk away. You then collect royalties, debate whether to let Guy Ritchie turn it into a movie, and pick out where you want to live now. That's probably the hardest part of the whole book-writing experience, deciding what to do with your money. Are you a beachfront cottage or mountain chalet person? That's the real dilemma of book writing. Picking your second home. Huge hassle."

That's the answer I used to want before I became a well-traveled, seasoned author of a grand total of three books. But you only have to publish one book and pursue your dream a little to learn a lesson about the unfortunate relationship between quantity and quality. It's a lesson that applies to every form of dream chasing.

Quantity leads to quality.

The more you practice your dream, the better you get at your dream.

In order to get a 50,000-word book published, I had to write 500,000 words on my blog. I had to essentially give away a half million words before I could build the momentum and ability to actually write the book. Since it came out, I've added another 500,000. So in three years, I've written one million words to publish 50,000.

And as I've mentioned, Stuff Christians Like wasn't the first blog I had. I had another one called Prodigal Jon for about a year before I even started SCL. Barely anyone read that one. But that was a testing ground for me. That gave me the chance to practice my dream.

Even that phrase looks weird, doesn't it? "Practice my dream." Nobody says that. Practice is for sports or GRE tests or things that are difficult. It's not a word we often associate with a dream. But I think it's a critical one if you really want to turn a day job into a dream job. There is much practice involved. There are Nebraska years and grinding it out and sweat and early mornings. And you have to commit to put quantity before quality.

You can't reverse those. If you try, analysis paralysis will cripple you. The false promise of perfection will keep you from pursuing your dream. Putting quantity first gives you the freedom to be patient with yourself. "This is the quantity portion of my dream. This is exactly where I'm supposed to be. These aren't mistakes I'm making, these are quantity payments. I'll get to quality, but first I have to pay the cost of quantity."

I wish this weren't true, for both our sakes. But if it were easy to execute a dream, everyone would do it and your dream wouldn't be so spectacular.

The fountain of free

There have been hundreds of articles and at least a dozen books written about the word *free* in the last ten years. With the growth of the internet and the abundance of free content, resources and wares, the opinion on whether or not you should give your dream away can be confusing. Some camps insist the best way to create fans is to give away whatever it is you're doing for a period of time with the hope that after that time you can charge a "freemium." You can see this approach executed in the "Light" version of Apple apps. I can download a free app, but it's only going to be a portion of the full-scale version of the app. I can play one level of a game, but to get to all levels, to get all of the Angry Birds, I have to upgrade to the paid version.

That's one line of thinking. The other says, "If you teach people not to value your dream from the beginning, they never will." The logic is that if you start out with a price tag of zero dollars, it's difficult to eventually charge money because when you tell someone your thing costs zero, they interpret it as worth zero. It becomes difficult for a fan to suddenly see monetary value in something initially valued at nothing.

I experienced this first-hand with Shazam. The app, not the Shaquille O'Neal movie. That was actually titled *Kazaam*. I can see how you might confuse the two. The Shazam app allows you to hold your iPhone up to any song playing anywhere and instantly get the name of it. When it first came out, Shazam would give you an unlimited number of song captures. I used to capture the title of about forty songs a month. It was free and I loved it. Then one day I tried to use the app and got a message that said I had used my allotted "tags" for the month. Unbeknownst to me, Shazam had reduced their infinite tags per month to five. That's a significant decrease. In order to make money, Shazam created a freemium version called Shazam Encore that costs $5.99. That's not a ton of money, and I completely get that Shazam is a for-profit company that has bills to pay, or it's an individual programmer who would like to trick out a loft like Tom Hanks in *Big*. But I never used the app again. I had a hard time mentally making the jump from "everything is free" to $5.99.

Your unique dream will likely require a creative approach to how you initially profit from it. But if you're going to hustle and you want to maximize the return, there will likely be at least some degree of freeness that comes up. Because the nature of transactional relationships has changed.

THREE THINGS I LEARNED ABOUT GIVING AWAY STUFF FOR FREE IN THE LAST THREE YEARS:

1. **People won't pay for what they can get for free.**
   One of the misconceptions about my first book is that it's just a printed version of the blog. It's not. I personally would never pay for a book version of something I already had access to online. That would be a really lazy, boring way to create a book.

   Stuff Christians Like has more than seventy new essays that have never been on the site and never will be. That's not to say that I didn't use some of the greatest hits from the site. I did. I thought of it like a concert. If you went to see U2 and they said, "Tonight we're going to sing all new songs from an album you haven't heard yet," you'd be disappointed. Even though you might love some of their new stuff, you want to sing along to "One" and "Where the Streets Have No Name" and a dozen of their other hits. That's how I looked at popular posts from my blog.

   People who liked the blog and picked up the book wanted to be able to flip to a page and show their friends "The Metrosexual Worship Leader Scorecard."

That was a greatest hit. I revised and updated it. And I included it in the book because it was a favorite.

I looked at the book as a continuation of the conversation I started for free on my blog. And even though I gave away a ton of free content online, I was still able to sell more than 40,000 copies of the book because it was not simply a photocopy of the blog.

I have a hard time believing people will pay for the exact same thing they can get for free. You have to change it, add to it, improve and in some way differentiate it if you're going to charge for it.

2. **You have to weigh the long-term benefits of doing something for free.**

Getting invited to speak at the Dave Ramsey headquarters for the first time was really exciting. I had barely spoken professionally before, and suddenly it felt like part of my dream was starting to gain momentum.

But as someone who was new to that arena, I didn't know if I should charge them for my visit. They hadn't mentioned an honorarium in their email to me. And I started to worry about what I should do:

"Is it better to charge Dave Ramsey for my speaking gig or not charge him? On the one hand, he's a financial guru and always talking about the need to take control of your money. Would he see me asking for money to cover my gas to Nashville from Atlanta as me being diligent with my budget? Or would they be insulted and say, 'Nevermind, we'll find someone else.' I can stay with my brother when I'm there, so my expenses will be minimal but it will definitely cost me a vacation day from work."

I went around and around in circles before ultimately deciding not to charge them. The experience was awesome and they graciously gave me a massive bag of books as a thank-you. Then a year later I spoke again for free. Then a year later I spoke again for free, but this time they bought a copy of my book for every staff member. That was a big deal. And it was after that third time that Dave offered me my dream job.

But what would have happened if, in 2008, as a no-name blogger without a book deal or any sort of real platform, I had fought for a $300 speaking honorarium? What if instead of hustling and coming up for free, I had pushed and scrapped to squeeze an extra few hundred dollars out of the situation? Those are great questions and I don't even have to give you a hypothetical answer. Here is what my team leader said would have happened: "We would have said, 'No thanks. We appreciate your responding to our request. Sorry that we couldn't make this one work out. We wish you the best on your future endeavors.'"

The relationship would have ended before it even really began. For $300 I would have put a stake in the heart of what would eventually become my dream job. That's a really expensive $300.

At the time of the decision on whether to charge, I didn't know I would work there as a full-time author and speaker two years later. I didn't have the vision to say, "I'll pass on this $300 so that I can have my dream job later." If life were that clear, we'd never make bad decisions. But as you face free-versus-charge decisions, do your best to weigh out the true cost of the money you might make. Is there a big potential long-term gain that could be ruined by your short-term gain? Is this a situation where you are undervaluing your dream and need to charge, or is it a chance to do something for free that might turn into something much bigger?

3. **Free pays dividends toward expertise**.
When we think about giving our dream away, we often worry about what we'll lose. Namely, money. If you do something for free, you do not get money. (I'm a pretty awesome economist.) But we sometimes lose sight of what we gain when we give our dream away.

Practice. Exposure. Audience. And eventually expertise.

When I thought about charging Dave Ramsey for my second professional speaking gig ever, I didn't have any of those things. I'd only spoken once before, so I needed the practice. I'd never spoken anywhere with name-brand recognition, so I needed the exposure of saying, "I'm speaking at the Dave Ramsey headquarters." And I'd never spoken to an audience that regularly communicated with a fan base of 4.5 million radio listeners, so I needed the audience of 300 influencers. My need for expertise greatly outweighed my need for $300. Even though I couldn't foresee that two years later I would gain my dream job from this same speaking opportunity, I could see that the gain in experience was worth more than the gain in finances. And because I still had a day job, I could afford not to charge for that gig. The Dons weren't going to get me, because I didn't quit my job the wrong way. My bills were covered.

That's not to say I didn't charge for speaking at the time. I got paid by a conference for the very first time I spoke professionally. They offered me an honorarium and I gladly accepted it. I want you to charge for your dream, and I love the stuff folks like Ben Arment, with Dream Year, do to help people figure out sustainable revenue models. But I want to make sure that when you wrestle with free you don't over-focus on the money you'll lose.

Jerry Seinfeld, the centerpiece of the most successful sitcom of all time, understands that principle. In an interview called "Jerry Seinfeld on Comedy," he discusses a time he was first working on his dream job of being a comedian. He did two shows a night for eighteen months straight without missing a night. That's over 1,000 shows.

Can you imagine how much money he made? The answer is none. Seinfeld says, "We weren't being paid. We had to work, to learn, to get good enough to get work."

One of the greatest comedians of all time had to give away his funny for free so he could gain enough experience to get paid for his dream job. Chances are, you will too.

Although I've been speaking professionally for three years, I will still do some gigs for free in support of this book. I'll prepare a speech for weeks, fly from Nashville to San Diego, do the absolute best job I can, and get paid zero dollars. Why? The success of this book matters more to me than the money I could make on the gig. I need the practice. I need the exposure. The book needs the audience. I'm not an expert yet and free pays me dividends toward that goal.

The beauties and dangers of competition

Speaking of Seinfeld, last Thanksgiving my family held a "Festivus Feats of Strength Contest."

We didn't intend to. We only planned to run a 5K Turkey Trot that morning. Nobody threw down the gauntlet of competition in the weeks leading up to the holiday. It was simply our year to get together as a whole family at a beach house. We expected nothing more than some quality family time. Relaxing, beach-style downtime.

Instead, we ended up in the midst of an elaborate, multi-event bloodfest that spanned all three days. It started with the Turkey Trot, which my youngest brother, Bennett, won. Then, as soon as there was some blood in the water, we all started to find new ways to compete. We held a 100-yard dash on the beach. We held a Frisbee distance-throwing contest. We held a heated game of billiards. And finally we held a "jump off the dock in November and swim back to shore" contest. Almost everything we did turned into a competition, save for our family game of cards.

We disqualified that game because my dad likes to teach us new card games and then slowly roll out rules at his leisure. In the middle of the game, as you get what you have been told is a winning hand, he will blurt out, "Ohhh, I forgot a rule. Sevens actually equal four in this game. My bad. Forgot to mention that." Convenient.

I'm very competitive, so when it came time to chase my dream, that sort of competition was in the back of my mind. It will probably be in yours too, since it's so easy to see who your competition is now.

Thirty years ago, if you wanted to be a freelance graphic designer, you couldn't easily find the other thirty graphic designers in your niche. There were conferences and organizations, but without the internet it was difficult to discover where you stood. Now there are a million ways to do that.

In three seconds, you can do a specific Google search and pull up all the websites of those you feel you might be competing against. You can read niche periodicals online. You can join forums and see who everyone refers to as the gold standard. You can see how many Twitter followers your competition has. You can check out their blog to see how often they update it, what new clients they secured, how strong their portfolio is and how many comments they get every day on a new post. In an afternoon you can get a virtual wheelbarrow of intel on your competition. That can be a great thing or a horrible thing depending on how you use it.

In my own experience with how competition can impact a dream, I've learned one critical thing: Competition is a great motivator but a horrible measurement.

I like to look at what other authors do on their blogs. Often they've thought of things I would have never imagined doing. I can find new ideas or approaches or a million other things that spark my creativity. Last Christmas, for instance, I looked at TonyMorganLive.com and saw that he did ten days of his top ten posts from the year. He used the content to take a ten-day break during the holidays instead of having to write new posts each day. I was initially planning to just do one post with ten links to my ten best posts. Instead, I tried Tony's method and was able to introduce ten days of content that a lot of people would have missed if I did it all as a single post.

There are times when looking at your competition will inspire you and encourage you. It's like going to a library of active projects. That's the beautiful potential of competition. Motivation.

But there is also a poison you have to be wary of: using competition as a form of measurement.

Pitting your dream against someone else's is a fantastic way to get discouraged and depressed. Nothing good comes from measuring your dream against your competition.

If you're beating them, by whatever arbitrary form of measurement you're using, you run the risk of getting cocky and lazy. Feeling ahead, you'll take a nap and relax like the hare racing the tortoise. If you're getting beat by them, you'll start to feel like a failure and think that maybe you might as well quit. Measuring yourself against the competition is a lose-lose prospect.

Even if you somehow manage to avoid either of those two paths, if you're the rare person who doesn't fall into one of those two results, measuring yourself against the competition is still fairly pointless. Comparing your unique dream against someone else's is like comparing apples and skateboards. The two will never measure up precisely.

I have to remember this truth all the time when I try to compare myself to MichaelHyatt.com.

Michael Hyatt is a friend who has a massive blog. It's also incredibly well-designed. When I look at his site and compare it to mine, I can instantly point out six ways I am failing but he is succeeding:

1. He makes it easy to sign up for his RSS feed.

2. His speaking dates scroll at the top so that people can see them.

3. He has graphics in his posts.

4. His YouTube channel is easy to find.

5. He's speaking at a lot of publishing events
   and I'm not.

6. He interviews really interesting authors via video.

His blog is better than mine in so many ways it makes my head spin. But here's the thing: He's the CEO of a major publishing company. He's a grandfather in his midfifties who has spent decades successfully leading businesses. He's an expert in the publishing field. Is that the goal of my dream? To work in publishing? To become a CEO? To run a massive company?

Not at all. I don't want to run a publishing company, I want to be published. There's a significant difference between my dream and his dream. But when I compare myself to him, I pretend there's not.

I don't know who or what you will compare yourself to when you start to hustle, but I promise you will find competition. That is a temptation that even the best of us can't resist. But when you do, let the competition serve as a source of motivation, not a source of measurement.

Then what should you measure?

Measuring your dream against someone else's is toxic but the idea of measuring progress is important. Without a way to measure what you're doing, you'll never really know how much your dream has grown as a result of all your hustle.

To not take measurements or track your progress would be like starting a diet and never stepping on the scale or getting your body fat measured. On days when you didn't feel like you were making any progress, you'd have no way to refute that feeling with data. We need data.

But what kind of data? Because some data is deadly. At least it was for me, and there's a counselor named Chuck who can verify that.

I might be the first person in the history of therapy to need a counselor because of blog statistics. In the first six months of working on the Stuff Christians Like blog, I got really fascinated by Google Analytics (GA). GA is a simple piece of code that will track any activity on your website. With a click of a button, you can instantly know how many unique visitors you had to your site, where they came from, what they read and how long they stayed. There are dozens, if not hundreds, of ways to measure everything on your blog. I believe I used them all.

At first it was okay. I would check in a few times every day to see if I was getting a lot of comments, see how the pageviews numbers were, and measure a few other key stats. I'd get a little hit of adrenaline every time I saw something spike on the graph and a little hit of depression every time something I wrote bottomed out.

I liked seeing the instant feedback so much that I started to check GA every few hours. Then every hour and then every few minutes. I started to see the statistics not as a measure of my blog traffic but as a measure of my self-worth. If the traffic was up, so was I. If it was down, so was I. I hit the refresh button on Firefox like a gambler pulling the lever of a slot machine.

Eventually, when my obsession reached a peak, I decided to go back to my counselor and talk about it. That was a weird conversation and went something like this:

Chuck the Counselor:
"You've created an army of idols."

Me:
"What do you mean, an army of idols?"

Chuck the Counselor:
"The readers of your site have become an army of idols for you. You're worshiping them and dependent on them to dictate how you feel. And they're always attacking."

Me [wishing I was saying something more intelligent in case this conversation made it into a book later]:
"How so?"

Chuck the Counselor:
"If your readers give you affirmation, if they leave nice comments or affirm you with good traffic, you misappropriate that and use it to feel better about yourself. So that's essentially an attack because you're using it to cripple your innate self-worth. If your readers leave you a hateful comment, that's a direct attack. In both ways,

you've set up a situation where you get attacked regardless of what happens."

Chuck the Counselor is smart because that's exactly what I did. If the traffic numbers weren't good when I posted in the morning, I would quickly write a new post for the afternoon, panicking that I was going to lose people. Instead of using the traffic as a tool, I let it become my master and responded accordingly depending on what the numbers said.

I thought that I was perhaps the only one who did this until I heard business guru and best-selling author Seth Godin address this in a conference. Someone asked him how many subscribers he had to his blog. He told them he didn't know. Because if he knew, he'd be tempted to make that number grow and he'd start to create content just to make the number grow. Then he said something that I think is so applicable to closing the gap between a day job and a dream job.

"You can't use analytics to figure out the message."

In other words, you can't allow your results or the measurement of your progress to control your dream. What you do, the message, so to speak, has to be true and honest and come from the core of what you care about, not be a whim in the whirling winds of analytics.

You might be better at this than I am. I'm not great at using analytics without getting all tangled in them. When I see that a post about Justin Bieber got the most traffic one month, I am tempted to write another post about Justin

Bieber. But that's not what I started out to do. I never felt called to high traffic numbers. I felt called to share my ideas. Those are two different things. So for the most part I now leave analytics alone. Thanks, Chuck.

When I do use them, I try to look at the progress of a month instead of a day or a week. Because when you get obsessed with measuring the progress of your dream, no matter what it is, you overestimate the importance of a day.

When I see traffic dip sharply on a Tuesday, it's easy to think the site is about to go under. But if I'm really committed to living out a fifty-year dream, if the canvas on which I am painting is five decades big, then a single Tuesday doesn't hold a lot of weight.

So if your dream is to open a restaurant, become a missionary, go back to school or anything else, what should you measure?

Measure hustle first.

I think measuring the effort you're putting in is a much more honest gauge of your progress. It's also the only part of this process you can really control. There are a million factors that play into getting traffic on a website or closing a sale or any other sign of a "hit" for your dream. There is only one who impacts the amount of hustle. You.

Measure the things you can control before the things can't. You can measure the number of days you got up early to work on your dream. You can measure the number of emails you responded to on your website. You can measure the number of dream jobs you applied for. That's what is going to matter at first. And if you set a high-hustle goal and miss it, you are rarely disappointed. You still made progress. If you miss a hit goal, you're far more affected.

My team leader set a huge, audacious sales goal for this book. If I miss it, if the book doesn't sell as many as we hoped, then we'll definitely have a conversation about that. He'll hold me accountable to that goal, but the first thing he'll really hold me accountable to is the hustle I put into making that goal happen.

We'll measure my hustle:

- Did I speak as often as I could have?

- Did I hold as many smart promotions on my blog as I could have?

- Did I write the best possible book I could have?

- When the PR team at work needed things from me, was I quick to respond?

- When the sales team needed information, did I give it to them right away?

- When a speech didn't work well, did I rewrite it so that it was better the next time?

These are the types of questions my boss will ask me, but they're also the questions I'll ask myself long before he calls a meeting.

If I miss a goal, which sometimes happens when you set huge ones, I want the reassurance that I did everything in my power to make it happen. I want the peace in knowing that is wasn't for lack of hustling that I missed a target for my dream. I want to know that the one thing in my control was under control.

I don't mean to say you should never measure your hits. You should. I did. We used Nielson BookScan to gauge book sales and observed blog traffic to pick out the best cities for my book tour. I believe there is tremendous value in measuring hits, but the point is a matter of priority.

Measure hits before hustle and you're likely to end up failing in more ways than one. Measure hustle before hits and the hits will come in due time. The next step is making sure you know what to do with that success.

CHAPTER 7

Learn to Be
Successful at Success

Robert Downey Jr. ruined my impression of what happens to you when you publish a book.

Well, he and Jodie Foster. Both had a part in crushing my childhood dreams. But if you see them, if you ever sit next to them on a flight, please don't bring the whole thing up. They'll pretend they don't know what you're talking about, but in your heart you'll know they know, and you'll probably be detained by TSA for starting an in-air celebrity feud.

There's a slim chance they don't remember what happened because they both make so many movies. I, on the other hand, have not forgotten.

Years ago, Jodie Foster directed a film called *Home for the Holidays* starring Downey Jr. It was an interesting movie based on a short story by a talented author named Chris Radant. So what, right? Wrong. There's a big "so what?" with Chris Radant.

I met her when I was writing branding and product descriptions at Bose. Prior to meeting her, I believed that if you wrote and published a book, from that moment on you slept on piles of money. Though I made fun of that perception earlier in the book, it was the perception I once had too. I thought success as an author meant an instant rapper-level existence. Gold teeth, rims of diamonds, lighting money on fire just to watch it burn, all pretty.

Chris Radant popped that wildly inaccurate expectation of my dream for me. She wrote the book *Home for the Holidays*. Not only did she write it, but the book got turned into a movie. Not just an art film where a symbolic glass of milk is broken in slow motion over cobblestones with someone speaking soft French in the background; her book was turned into a big Hollywood movie directed by Jodie Foster. In addition to the dump truck of cash you get for writing a book, she should have gotten a second dump truck of cash for the movie.

She didn't.

She was doing the exact same job I was at Bose. We were both in the same size cubicles with the same responsibilities and the same corporate expectations. Was something wrong with Chris? Did she do a horrible job managing all her author cabbage? Nope.

She was an incredibly talented author who worked hard on her craft. There was nothing wrong with Chris. Something was wrong with me. I had grossly failed to define what success looks like for a writer. I had greatly misinterpreted what success looks like for a dream. And it cost me years of frustration. Years that I'd prefer you not go through.

It's time to define

If I were an NFL player, one of my goals each year would be to stay out of news stories that involved me and the phrase "outside a night club." Forget the injuries you receive out on the field, battling against 300-pound giants. The most dangerous place on the planet for a professional athlete is outside a night club.

For those of us without a lucrative contract with an NFL team, the space outside a nightclub isn't that deadly. But if you're going to chase your dream, there is another space you need to be careful of.

Success.

It sounds ironic, but more dreamers fail in success than they do in failure. Success is like the Bermuda Triangle of dreams. There are two primary reasons.

The first is that we tend to only view success as a good thing. We plan a million ways not to fail. We erect processes against failure and establish backup plans if things go wrong.

We don't spend nearly as much time, if any at all, safeguarding ourselves from success. We strive for success. We reach for it. We yearn for it. We aim for it with everything we've got. And when we get a taste of it, we're often woefully unprepared for the challenges that come.

The attention, the opportunities, the desire for people to tell you what you want to hear instead of what is true. All these multiply with success. You need to be prepared.

The other reason success is so dangerous is that we get arrogant. No one gets cocky when they fail. No one ever says, "That guy failed so badly that he got really full of himself and ended up alienating everyone in his life." Arrogance only runs with success. And it's dangerous.

Author Malcolm Gladwell summarized this problem in a speech he gave: "Incompetence irritates me, but overconfidence scares me. Incompetent people rarely have the opportunities to make mistakes that greatly affect things. But overconfident leaders and experts have the dangerous ability to create disaster."[14]

He was specifically referring to the business leaders who contributed to the housing market and credit collapse of 2008–2009. But he spoke a truth that applies to even the smallest dream.

When you're dreaming alone in a cubicle at work, you have very little ability to really impact things. But when you start working on your dream, overcoming risks and hustling, you'll start to gather some momentum. You might not run a company of 10,000 people but, as a mom or dad, your dream decisions will greatly impact the lives of your children. As a single adult, your actions can have a surprising impact on the friends and family members who are cheering you on. If your dream involves giving back to your community or another country, whole parts of the world can be affected by what you do.

And with the internet and social media, your ability to, as Gladwell explains, "create disaster" is only amplified. It only takes a handful of followers on Twitter or Facebook to get cocky. It only takes a few blog comments or purchases of your widget to feel like you're Leonardo DiCaprio on the bow of the Titanic, which might be a more accurate metaphor than you realize. As Jimmy Fallon, host of the *Late Show*, described his movie failures after his successful run on *Saturday Night Live*, "You start thinking you're awesome, when the truth is, you're not."[15]

But isn't success what we're aiming for? I didn't start my blog with the hope that it would fall flat. I didn't write my books with the expectation that I could sell them slightly better than the average author. Not at all. I want you to be successful with your dream. I want all of us to be successful. I just don't want your success to kill your dream, which is why there's one critical thing you have to do before you get successful.

Define your "enough"

When the Stuff Christians Like blog took off, I got nervous. All of a sudden people were telling me I was special and interesting and smart and a whole lot of other things I'd never had groups of strangers tell me. I wasn't ready for it. I started to feel the tendrils of arrogance wrapping around my ankles. I started writing the blog with an almost maniacal level of focus. It became my obsession and started to cost me relationships. As a stopgap for that, I decided to interview leaders who seemed to have it all together. Some would meet with me for coffee; some blew me off, because despite thinking I was important, I had only a mildly successful niche blog. On the success ladder I was very, very, very low.

One of the leaders who agreed to meet with me was Lanny Donoho, a comedian/author/camp founder/hybrid of an entertainer. We sat in his office one afternoon, an octagon-shaped room in an old Victorian house in Alpharetta, Georgia. On most of the eight walls he had big boards with ideas blocked out on colorful Post-it notes. It felt like being inside *Saturday Night Live*.

I told him I was worried about what was happening with the modicum of success I was experiencing and he told me a story. Here, in a complete paraphrase because I had no idea how important this conversation would become and certainly did not scribble it down lightning fast like a squirrel at the time, is what he said:

"Jon [people in stories you remember always say your name but never usually do in real life], have you ever used 'futureme.org'? It's a site where you can send yourself emails in the future. You can write an email today and post it so that it comes to you in a week, a month, a year, whenever. I did that a year ago. I was working on a project that was killing me. The money was great. The opportunity was huge, but it was literally killing me. I was ill and stressed out and so unhappy. In that moment, a year ago, I fortunately had the clarity to send myself a message in the future. A few weeks ago I found myself on the doorstep of another big opportunity. The money was great, the project was huge and I was about to take it, when a message from Lanny Donoho to Lanny Donoho showed up. Know what it said? 'Don't take projects like this ever again. You're in pain right now, getting crushed by this project. If you ever have a chance to take this type of project again, be careful. Say no. Please.' I had forgotten all about that situation. I had moved on and was about to jump back into that same type of situation. But I didn't because the me from a year ago sent a message to the me of today."

At the time I thought Lanny was being a little silly. I once saw him bring a live camel into a conference, so silly is definitely in his wheelhouse. But since I felt like I was drowning at the time, I tried it. I was wrong about Lanny's advice.

It was an amazing experience. There is something really powerful about writing yourself a letter in the future. It forces you in an unexpectedly creative way to wrestle with what you really want out of life. It makes you strip away a lot of your layers and get down to some of your core truths.

On April 12, 2009, having just finished writing the *Stuff Christians Like* book, I sent myself an email a year before it would release. At the time I worked at AutoTrader.com. I wouldn't move to Nashville and take the Dave Ramsey job for another 16 months. Here is an excerpt of the email I received from myself on March 3, 2010.

Dear Jon,
The book Stuff Christians Like *has probably released at this point. It's March and you might be tempted to run around like crazy saying yes to every opportunity to speak*

and be interviewed and write. (Or maybe there aren't any, who knows.)

But in the midst of this time I want you to remember that a few weeks ago (in March 2009) you sat outside with Jenny on the side of your house in the brown adirondack chairs with the sun setting and you thought to yourself, "This is enough. I have a beautiful wife, a house to live in, two wonderful children, a job. This is enough. There's no reason to chase money or material possessions when the book comes out. I have enough."

Remember that, in case you are tempted right now to think you've got to compromise your life in some sort of way to sell more copies of the book. It's just a book; it's not going to deliver you some sort of wonderful life. God has already done that.

Stay brave, stay contrarian, stay Jon Acuff.

In the middle of March 2010, that email showed up in my inbox. I had long forgotten it. I was in the center of a very noisy time. People were telling me to quit my job that second. Opportunities were multiplying like small fluffy rabbits. I was deep, deep into chase mode. And there was one word in that email that almost a year later I can't stop thinking about.

It's not my misspelled version of *Adirondack* (no double *o* and lowercase *a*). The word that stood out to me was *enough*. The whole email was pretty convicting, but that word wouldn't let me go.

Enough.

As in, "It's enough."

As in, "You have enough, don't let the dream you're chasing blind you to the life you already have."

As in, "Success will tell you that your enough is not enough, and it will keep you on a treadmill of your own design, but a treadmill nonetheless."

That to me is the key to being successful at success. Instead of chasing "enough," you have to define it. If you chase it, you'll never catch it. Enough is incredibly quick. Much like perfection, it seems to remain out of reach.

"As soon as we sell $1,000,000 worth of products, we'll have enough business."

"As soon as I hit 20,000 comments on my blog, I'll have enough to feel good about my platform."

"As soon as I make partner, or executive or _____, I'll have enough freedom to take some time off."

But we often never reach enough when we chase it.

On the other hand, you are guaranteed to get to enough when you define it. You only find enough when you tell enough where to be found.

Former Lakers coach Pat Riley touched on the problem of enough in his book *Show Time*. He called it "the disease of more" and asserted, "Success is often the first step toward disaster."[16] NBA Hall of Famer Isiah Thomas elaborated on that problem in his own basketball experience. In Cameron Stauth's book *The Franchise*, he says, "A team wins [a championship] one year and the next year every player wants more minutes, more money, more shots. And it kills them … But it's hard not to be selfish. The art of winning is complicated by statistics, which for us becomes money."[17]

The disease of more transcends teams and is true of all of us as individuals. The first taste of success, of winning, awakens the giant of enough. And if it's not already defined, it will grow out of control.

Before you get hit with that first wave of success, sit down with a piece of paper or a futureme.org email and define what your enough will look like.

I am still learning this lesson.

This week I wrote myself an email that I will receive a year from now. I wrote about this book. I wrote about my faith and my family. I continued to define my enough.

I hope this book is extremely successful. I hope you give it to everyone you know. I hope that it sells 100,000 copies and changes lives all over the world. But I'm not going to wait for that success to tell me the whole experience is enough.

I've already defined that.

Don't burn out

When we talk about chasing our dreams and successfully doing more of what we love with our lives, we often throw caution to the wind. We work until we drop and shrug off rest as something people who don't have our dream do. We "burn the candle at both ends."

I was curious about that phrase and looked it up. My expectation was that it was penned by a poet who lived a fast, dangerous life, smoking hand-rolled cigarettes and writing on scrolls. I was right in believing it was from a poem. I was wrong about the poet. Edna St. Vincent Millay said it.

Here is what she wrote:

> *I burn my candle at both ends,*
> *It will not last the night.*
> *But ah, my foes, and oh, my friends,*
> *It gives a lovely light.*

When I read that, I assumed that was one of Edna's only poems, the speed and intensity of her light burning out quickly. I couldn't have been more mistaken. She actually wrote for decades. She was no one-hit wonder, but instead won the Frost Award for her lifetime contribution to American poetry. She's a legend in the poetry world.

But I fear we've twisted her words. We've treated that line about burning a candle at both ends as if it's prescriptive, not descriptive. As if the best sign of real success is burning out. Burnout is a badge of honor. Exhaustion is the mark of excellence.

No one sets out to kill their dream through exhaustion, but it often happens because dreams are ravenous. They will take all the time you give them. They will swallow relationships and other priorities and anything in their radius if you allow them to burn both ends of your candle.

I didn't realize this had happened to me until we moved away from Atlanta.

One night, a week before we moved, my wife and I were sitting outside in our Adirondack chairs. My wife asked me, "Who of your good friends in Atlanta will you really miss?" She asked me that because she had a pretty extensive list.

Lori was like her sister. Katie was down the street and vital to her. Leanne was developing into one of her best friends. For thirty minutes she went through a great collection of "heart friends" she was going to miss when we moved to Nashville.

I had a hard time coming up with my list. It's not that I didn't have friends. I did. I ate breakfast with a guy named Matt every other week for four years. I was starting to hang out with my friend Mark from our neighborhood. But to be honest with you, I didn't have many deep heart friends because I didn't invest in relationships once Stuff Christians Like took off. Prior to the success of the blog, I met regularly with a group of men I loved. I had great friendships that I actively invested in every week. Then the site blew up and I stopped investing in friendships.

Relationships take time and if you don't feed them they tend to die. But I was so in love with my dream of writing and so convinced I had to burn the candle at both ends, I wasn't willing to feed my friendships. Any free time I had went to developing the blog. In the mornings, at night, on the weekends, I was writing, writing, writing.

If my wife and kids would go out of town for the weekend, I usually wouldn't connect with anyone. I would sit at home, writing blog entries, answering emails or growing my Twitter list. I didn't put relationships in the right place on my "like vs. love list." For two and a half years I did this, until we moved to Nashville and I realized I didn't have many people who would miss me.

Burn your dream bright. Pursue it with the best of who you are. But don't confuse hustle with burnout. Hustle fills you up. Burnout empties you. Hustle renews your energy. Burnout drains it. Hustle impacts every other aspect of your life in a positive way as you learn to prioritize the things that matter. Burnout impacts every other aspect of your life in a negative way as your dream becomes the only thing that matters.

Don't accept burnout as the price or definition of success. It is neither. My site might have succeeded, but I paid for it with my friendships.

The land of later is a myth

"I've got to put in the crazy hours at work right now so that eventually we'll be able to have the life we want for our kids."

A friend told me that once. He was in the middle of a season where he was working fourteen-hour days. He'd get up in the dark, come home in the dark, and squeeze his family in there somewhere between coming home at seven and collapsing into bed at eight. From the outside, it was easy to see that he was killing his family in the name of pursuing his dream job.

Though it's easy to judge that person in the pages of a book or when we see it in someone else's life, the reality is that situations like that first take root from a very noble place.

As moms and dads, husbands and wives, maybe even as sons and daughters, we all want to provide. We want to give everything we have to make sure our family has anything they need. That's a great desire I would never criticize. But it gets compromised when we make the mistake of believing in later.

What my friend was really saying to me was, "I have to work like crazy right now, so my family can be better off *later*."

The problem is that kids don't believe in later. As parents we might think that in a few years, when they're older, our kids will appreciate and maybe even understand the long hours we put into following our dreams and working, but they don't. Kids believe in right now. That's the only reality they understand.

I've never heard a 13-year-old say, "My dad really wasn't around for the first ten years of my life, but I have a really nice bike now, so it all evens out."

Kids don't say that. They might not have the ability to verbally communicate what it means to be lonely as a 6-year-old, but they are when we ignore them for the sake of pursuing our dreams in order to create a better later.

It's not just kids who don't believe in later. Spouses don't believe in it either. I promise you that during the first year of having the blog Stuff Christians Like blow up, my marriage didn't get better. I cocooned myself within that dream and pursued it the wrong way, shutting my wife out of the experience. I put her in the last place you want your spouse to be, on the opposite side of your dream.

When she would say, "I feel like you're spending too much time on your blog," I would hear, "I want your dream to fail." I would knee-jerk respond and say things like, "This is what I was created to do. This is my purpose. Why do you hate my dream?" (I am not anticipating the arrival of the Husband of the Year trophy on my doorstep anytime soon.) I made her an opponent of my dream instead of a partner. And it's a surprisingly easy place to arrive when you start obsessing about your dream right now, in the hopes of a better later.

I once heard comedian Louis CK discuss this on the Marc Maron podcast. Louis CK's comedy is brilliant but incredibly vulgar. So when I heard him talk about why dreamers sometimes get divorced, it caught me completely off guard. Here is what he said:

> I had seen a lot of *60 Minutes* episodes where they talk about a guy like Bill Parcels or whoever and you just look at how he's so manic and so amazing. And then they talk to his wife and she always has this kind of smile and says, "We just

know that we don't see Bill from September 1
to February 15 and that's, you know, you make
a deal with yourself that that's okay and I love
him." And then at the end of the episode Morly
Safer says, "And they're divorced now."

This isn't an "if" scenario. It is a "when" scenario. If
you chase your dream the wrong way and get lost in the
land of later, you will lose relationships. With your kids,
with your spouse and with your friends.

Cue mournful trumpet: *whaaa waaaa.*

But there is a way to destroy the land-of-later myth.
And it's actually really simple.

You do the math.

I learned this idea watching my friend Dwayne deal
with the success metrics of being an accountant. After he
hurt his family working a ton of hours, he decided to scale
back from being the 7 a.m. to 7 p.m. guy and start working
from 7 a.m. to 4 p.m.

Although the lines got a little blurred during tax season,
he held strong to keeping his true time commitment
at home instead of at work. The result was fairly expensive.

In his first annual review, his manager told him that
they were happy with his performance except for one thing,
his time management. While everyone else at the company
had spent fifty-plus hours of work at the office, Dwayne
had averaged forty.

The cost of that time difference was going to be
reflected in his annual bonus. The bonus had been reduced
by $2,000 to reflect Dwayne's decision to work less.

Now, for Dwayne, someone whose dream is accounting, $2,000 felt like an expensive penalty to pay. Had he just worked harder on his dream, he could have had $2,000 more of success. You'll get into similar situations as you get successful too. Regardless of the specifics of your dream, there will always be just a little bit more success out of reach. And if you don't do the math, you'll think you're missing out.

But here's what happened when I asked Dwayne to stop and do the math.

After taxes, $2,000 only translates to about $1,500. And if he had only worked 10 more hours a week for an entire year, he would have received that money. So the equation is simple: His company offered him $1,500 for 500 hours of his time, or approximately $3 per hour. So Dwayne decided that hanging out with his wife and daughter was worth $3 an hour. He decided that if someone offered to sell him ten more hours a week with his family for only $30, he would buy it. In a heartbeat.

So he didn't lose $2,000. He paid $3 an hour to get to know his daughter during a period of her life that is fleeting and fast. Would you make the same decision? I hope so.

Now clearly, the math in Dwayne's situation was easy. Yours might be more complicated. The opportunities more tempting. The siren's call of the land of later even louder. But the principle holds true. If we'll take the time to hit pause and consider the true cost and true gain of a "little more success" with our dream, we'll often be surprised at the real numbers.

Don't turn your platform into a prison

When you get successful at your dream, you're going to acquire something: a platform.

This is an important word that is only going to become more important as more people chase their dreams. A platform is the spot you dream from. It's your blog, your audience, your readers, your shoppers, as Godin would say, "your tribe."

It's already becoming increasingly difficult to get a book published without a platform, for instance. Ten years ago, no one asked you how many Twitter followers you had when you sent them your book proposal, but with so many people swimming in the same pool, it's critical to have a platform that can differentiate you from everyone else. And it's not just writers who need platforms. The same principle applies to every type of dream from writing to starting a small business. Fifteen years ago if you had a website for your business, you were unique. Now, if your company doesn't have an active Twitter account, Facebook strategy and blog plan, your platform is underdeveloped.

The problem with a platform is that if you don't build it the right way, it will become a prison. And one of the best ways to prevent this from happening is to share it.

I used to get jealous of people who wrote guest posts on my blog. Although my posts would normally get more comments, there was a part of me that would internally think, *Oh no, that person is getting popular. This is your blog. You better write something really funny or clever tomorrow, or people will leave your platform in droves.* This is a silly, insecure thing to think, but it happens to the best of us. Especially when you first get successful.

When you start building the platform of your dream, it's easy to get greedy. It never starts out that way but usually begins with you saying, "I need to protect my dream and my brand." You make some good decisions about how you'll live your dream, what your dream will stand for, who will be part of it, etc. And those are smart things to wrestle through. But if you put your arms around your dream too tightly, you'll start to be like a little kid who says "mine" over a pile of toys, and soon you won't have anyone to play with. Squeeze too tightly and you choke your dream.

If you're afraid to share the platform with someone else, you'll eventually be afraid to leave it at all. And that's really the definition of a prison, a place you can't leave. Not only will you become a convict of your dream; when you refuse to share it, you guarantee that your dream will begin and end with you.

I want us to have multi-generation dreams. To have a legacy that is bigger than our individual lives and actions. I don't want us to have selfish, "me-sized" dreams. I want us to have people who can dream alongside us, add their unique ideas and grow something that is bigger than we could ever do alone. That's a need we'll all express at one point: "I want to be part of something bigger than me."

You can actually be part of the catalyst for that type of movement, which is simply a dream inside a community, if you'll share it. If you'll be willing to have other people in the spotlight of your dream. If you won't clutch your dream and its platform too tightly.

Don't for a second interpret that as an urging to throw wide the gates of your dream and lose control of it to anyone and everyone who enters. I've gotten a lot better at sharing the platform of my blog. I've introduced other writers to publishers and tried to do my best to share my platform with writers who don't have one. But I don't accept every guest post request I get because the blog has a specific concept. It's a satire of faith that must be funny without being mean. So if someone submits a serious guest post about her cat dying and the critical lessons from the Old Testament the experience taught her, I don't post it. If someone submits a guest post about ways to get financial aid at Christian colleges, I don't post it. If someone submits a funny post that attacks a well-known minister, I don't post it.

Sharing your dream doesn't mean being stupid with it. You can kill a dream's platform by doling it out too often just as easily as you can by hoarding it. I wish there were an exact line between those two risks, but like so many other things in life, there's not. It's a balancing act. But if you're deliberate about the way you share, and you recognize your role in helping other people close the gap between their day jobs and dream jobs, you'll figure it out a lot faster than I did.

The yes side of no

In the first chapter I said that one of the benefits of not quitting your job is that you get to say no to the wrong opportunities. You get to turn down things because most, if not all, of your basic needs are taken care of by your day job. The flip side to that idea is that when you get successful, you'll have the chance to say yes to more opportunities.

Which is a great thing. When you get momentum, new opportunities come out of the woodwork. People start to slowly recognize your success and will give you the chance to do things you never knew were possible. But there are also ways to make a mess of your yes.

I was able to dodge the yes bullet when I took my dream job at Ramsey, but only because my team leader is smarter than I am.

One afternoon my friend Chris and I started brainstorming new opportunities. I'm paid in part on commission. So my family eats well and wears tuxedos when I do speaking gigs, sell books and secure advertising for my blog, among a few other things. Chris and I were trying to think of new ways to create some events. After reading an article about a young speaker who taught people how to be a speaker, I told Chris, "Why don't we hold a conference where I teach people how to publish a book?"

We got excited about that idea and started to throw ideas on the wall. We already have our own conference center here, so we wouldn't need to rent space. We could advertise on the radio since Dave Ramsey is on 450 stations. We could talk about it on Twitter and my blog. The speed and momentum of this idea started to build.

We put together a proposal for the head of our department and then pitched it to him. He listened to our idea, heard all the potential benefits we saw in this opportunity and then told us to "wait." He didn't kill the idea. He didn't praise the idea. He just said wait.

A month later I learned why he wanted us to wait.

It was a dumb idea. I've published one book traditionally and two others through Dave Ramsey's company. What do I know about publishing? I don't have a long track record to teach from. At the time we pitched the idea I had been a published author for all of eight months. Wow, that is an extensive history. I'm like Simon, the funnier brother in the Simon & Schuster team.

What, for a price, did I think I could offer people who are hanging their dreams on trying to get published? Eight months of experience? We were talking about putting on an eight-hour conference. That would have been an awkward seven and a half hours after I exhausted the thirty minutes of knowledge I had about publishing.

Could we have done it? Probably. Could we have pulled it off? Probably. Could we have made money on it and maybe even given out some helpful information? Probably. But in saying yes to that opportunity I would have taken a huge step toward becoming someone I don't want to be. I don't want to be a publishing expert; I want to be published. I'm more than happy to share things I learn along the way with people, but I'm not aspiring to be an expert on the publishing industry. I'm not a great linear thinker. If we need to move three cars around in our driveway, it takes me eighty-seven moves. I hate writing "how-to" material. I've never wanted to be a teacher and would be miserable trying to lead people through the process of publishing.

And although it might look like an opportunity, maybe even a well-paid opportunity, saying yes to the wrong thing ultimately takes you one step away from doing what you really want to do.

I didn't realize how important this problem was until I called my friend and mentor Mike Foster. I told him I was thinking about starting a small group for a few friends of mine, called "Don't Mess Up," or DMU. I had a handful of friends with blossoming writing careers, music careers and dream jobs. After seeing countless dreamers blow it in epic ways, I wanted to start a support group that would help us all navigate success. In response he told me:

"I think that's a great idea, but be careful that you don't just focus on the obvious ways to mess up: affairs, money, booze, porn, etc. I think one of the easiest ways you can mess up is by becoming someone you didn't intend to be. And that starts with the opportunities you decide to pursue."

He was right. It's incredibly easy, in the midst of some success, to say yes to the wrong things. To take small steps and big leaps away from the dream you defined in the second chapter. I promise there are dreamers out there who woke up fifteen years down the road and said, "How did I get here? When did I go so far off the course?" The reason this happens, the reason Mike is dead-on about the danger of opportunities, is that they never look like bad things at the outset. An affair, on the other hand, is bad from the get-go. You might lie to yourself about your intentions but it's difficult to dress up an affair as anything other than what it is: infidelity.

An opportunity that might not be good for you? That always looks good at first. You tell yourself things like, "I'll be able to expand my dream to a new audience. This will help my dream mature and stretch. It's a great opportunity and is just a job."

Do you hear the danger in that last sentence? It sounds a lot like what we told ourselves in the beginning of this book. It feels like we're widening the gap between our day job and our dream job.

By saying yes to the wrong things, you might actually be going backward, turning your dream job into something you never intended it to become. Sure, there will be times when you have to do things you don't like to earn money to fund doing the things you love. There's no such thing as a "perfect job" where you just do everything you love 100 percent of the time. That's why it's called a dream job, not a perfect job. But be very, very careful. Saying yes to the wrong things is a slippery slope that can lead you right back to the front of this book.

Don't erase all the good work you've done in the name of insignificant successes. Don't become a publishing expert if your dream is to be published. Allow your dream room to evolve but don't let it lead you away from your core desire. Don't say yes to the wrong opportunities.

How? By asking a simple question when you face new opportunities: ["If I say yes to this opportunity and am successful at it, what will be the long-term outcome?"]

Let's use me as an example.

If Chris and I were to create that "How to Publish" conference and it were successful, what would happen? We'd probably make decent money, which would be hard to say no to. And if people were happy with it, they'd tell their friends they should do it too. We'd probably be able to do more conferences and maybe I'd get asked to speak at publishing events. Maybe I'd even get to write a book about getting published. If I was *successful* at it, which is the key word in that question, the outcome would be a whole lot more opportunities to speak about publishing. And therein lies the trap.

The reward of getting really good at something less significant than your real dream is that you get to do it more often. That's not a reward; that's a punishment. The goal of this entire book is to lead you into doing more of what you love doing, or precisely the opposite of what will happen if you're successful at doing stuff you don't love.

I'm going through that same situation right now with public speaking. I love public speaking. I enjoy it as much as writing. I consider it a big part of my dream. But I have to be extra careful about saying yes to the wrong opportunities. Because I had a little success at a few conferences, I'm getting more opportunities. If I say yes to all of them, it won't take long for me to wake up and realize I'm somebody I never dreamed of becoming. The absentee father.

That's how I felt waking up in a hotel room in the Midwest alone one morning last fall. During a stretch when I was out of town seven of eight weekends, I got lost in the middle of my dream. I failed to ask my own question: "If I say yes to this opportunity and I am successful at it, what will be the long-term outcome?"

The outcome of being a successful speaker, if you carry the thread out long enough, is that you get to be on the road 200 days of the year. That's not my dream. Being away from my family is so far from the core of my dream, yet it's easy to see how I could get there.

I plan on becoming the best public speaker I can possibly be. I plan to work on that and hustle on that and be faithful to that part of my dream. But along the way, I plan to not say yes to the wrong opportunities.

Dreaming beyond success

Ken Bradshaw is a 58-year-old big-wave surfer. He rides building-sized swells all over the world and in 1998 rode the largest wave ever surfed. It was eighty-five feet tall. I read an interview with him once and a lot of the piece focused on the decisions he's made in life that fly in the face of how most people would define surfing success.

He doesn't have any big-name sponsors. He doesn't enter many contests. The author of the article said Bradshaw referred to one of the biggest events in surfing as a contest "about selling beachwear to landlocked dreamers in Iowa." He has made far, far less money than Kelly Slater, who is often thought of as the Michael Jordan of surfing. Reading that paragraph, it's easy to judge Bradshaw as a failure. That would be a mistake.

Bradshaw wasn't unsuccessful. He was wildly successful based on his own definition of success. At the end of the article, the author asks him if he has any regrets about the choices he's made. Bradshaw responds, "My life is full of 'my faults,' because I chose passion over industry."

And a "my fault" is not the same as a regret.[18]

I love this description. A "my fault" is when you define success differently than the popular definition. It's a healthy, responsible acknowledgment that "I could have experienced greater success, sure. But I haven't by my own choice. And I'm okay with that."

A regret is when you don't define your dream or your "enough," and you end up drifting someplace you never intended, never desired, to go. That comes with lots of regret.

If you've made it to this part of the book, you're done with regret. You're done being afraid of the obstacles between your day job and your dream job. You're done with other people's definitions of success. And, depending how far along you are right now, you might just be done with your day job too.

CHAPTER 8

Quit Your Day Job

Eventually, I quit my day job.

Despite having learned to appreciate the many things it offered and provided. Despite having fallen in like with a job I didn't love, I eventually gave my two weeks' notice. I wrote it out on a piece of paper and held an "I'm clearly quitting" meeting. Unless you do what I did to Derek at Staples and throw a quitting grenade, most bosses know when you're about to turn in your notice.

"Hey, I was just thinking, let's get together for thirty minutes or so on Friday at, say, 4:30 in the afternoon. Why? No reason, just want to hang out, talk about a few things. What? Noooo, you don't need to prepare anything in advance. There's no agenda."

That's not suspicious at all. Can't an employee unexpectedly schedule a meeting with his boss and bring a single sheet of paper to that meeting while sweating profusely without someone getting suspicious? Doubtful.

If you've been deliberate and smart about how and why you're going to quit, the boss is usually expecting it. If, on the other hand, things are being thrown and you're kicking over whatever it is a barista would choose to kick over in a fit of rage, that's not the type of exit I'm talking about. Although I wouldn't mind seeing that.

I'm talking about an intentional two weeks' notice. You've transitioned from not impulsively quitting your job to falling in like with a job you don't love to starting small and slow on your dream. The question now is, how do you know if you're really ready to quit your day job? This scorecard is probably the easiest way to figure it all out.

THE "ARE YOU REALLY READY TO QUIT YOUR DAY JOB?" SCORECARD

1. You've patiently worked through your plan to quit and honed the dream you really want to pursue for more than a month. = *+1 point*

2. You've patiently worked through your plan to quit and honed the dream you really want to pursue for more than six months. = *+2 points*

3. You've patiently worked through your plan to quit and honed the dream you really want to pursue for more than a year. = *+3 points*

4. You've been thinking about quitting for about an hour and worked on your dream over a long weekend a few months ago at Sully's lake house. = *-10 points*

5. You've already made the most of your nights and weekends, pursuing your dream with every available free moment you have. = *+2 points*

6. You pursue your dream in between episodes of reality shows or when the mood strikes you. = *-10 points*

7. Realizing your dream will require instant celebrity delivered via a wildly popular YouTube clip involving a double rainbow or a talking dog. = *-5 points*

8. You know a guy who did something similar to what you want to do and it seemed pretty easy. = *-4 points*

9. You apprenticed with that guy for a few months and learned your dream job is not easy, but definitely possible. = *+4 points*

10. You've built up an emergency fund that can handle three months of not having a steady salary. = *+1 point*

11. You've built up an emergency fund that can handle six months of not having a steady salary. = *+2 points*

12. Your financial plan is completely dependent on your car never breaking down. = *-1 point*

13. Or your rent going up. *= -2 points*

14. Or people expecting Christmas presents, in December this year. *= -2 points*

15. Your financial plan is completely dependent on your kids "living safe" and not getting a stomach virus or anything else that becomes painfully expensive when you have no health insurance. *= -5 points*

16. You've built a blog and are growing an active community that is engaged in helping you with your dream. *= +2 points*

17. You're thinking about getting on "the Facebook" or possibly "the Tweeter" one of these days. *= 0 points*

18. Your spouse is completely supportive of your decision. *= +5 points*

19. Every time you bring up the idea of quitting, your spouse throws up a little in his or her mouth. *= -3 points*

20. You've used the phrase "Why won't you let me follow my dream?" *= -1 point for each time you said it*

21. You've ever thought, *I'm not married, Acuff, and I have no kids. Enough with playing favorites, you half-dead 35-year-old. = Fair enough. Moving on.*

22. You've got a clear sense of what your dream looks like and know the next few steps to pursue it.
= +3 points

23. You kind of want to be a ballerina or maybe an astronaut or a racecar driver. *= -5 points*

24. Although you're nervous and perhaps a little scared about writing your two weeks' notice letter, you feel good about the decision. *= +2 points*

25. You are writing your quitting letter with such fury that you broke the *Q* on your keyboard.
= -10 points

26. Your backup financial plan if things take longer than you expect is to get a night job and hustle as hard as you can. *= +5 points*

27. Your backup financial plan if things take longer than you expect is to win the lottery, capture a leprechaun, or find some pirate's booty inexplicably buried in the landlocked state you live in. *= -10 points*

28. You skipped to this chapter without reading the rest of the book, because you knew instantly, "I'm ready to quit. I know I am." *= -50 points*

29. You've made a list of the things that are at risk if you quit and you are willing to put those things in jeopardy. *= +10 points*

30. "Risk" is what negative people worry about. I'm living in the now. Let's just do this thing already! *= -5 points*

31. You write dark, German punk metal–inspired poetry about how much you hate your job, but have not taken any productive steps toward making your dream happen. *= -5 points*

32. Your dream job is so different from your day job that there's no way your boss or company would ever help you achieve it. *= +5 points*

33. You love your day job and actually figured out how it can be a great place from which you can continue pursuing your dream for years and years. *= -10 points*

34. You love your job and just picked up this book because you keep hearing that the author is really handsome and wanted to see for yourself. *= -20 points*

35. You have a support network of friends and family members who will help you pursue your dream. = *+3 points*

36. Your friends and family don't completely understand your dream but they respect the maturity you've shown in pursuing it and are on board. = *+5 points*

37. Everyone else on the planet is crazy! What do they know about my dream? I'm the last known wise person alive. No one can add a shred of advice to my dream. = *-5 points*

38. You've ever said the phrase "Haters gonna hate!" when receiving any feedback that is critical of your dream. = *-5 points*

39. You've put together a detailed description of what your new workdays are going to look like. = *+3 points*

40. Your plan for your new workday involves you "listening to your heart" and "just seeing where the wind takes you." = *-5 points*

41. You've been seeing a professional counselor who gave you some great advice. = *+2 points*

42. You've been seeing a psychic who gave you some great warnings about something involving a raccoon and a tire iron. = *-5 points*

43. You're aware that you'll probably work harder than you've ever worked when you quit your day job and follow your dream. = *+2 points*

44. You look forward to all the free time you'll have when you follow your dream. = *-3 points*

45. You feel this is a decision that is in line with your core values or faith. = *+2 points*

46. For this to succeed, you'll need God to perform a miracle on par with the parting of the Red Sea. At least once a week. = *-5 points*

47. You've been working toward this moment for months if not years. = *+3 points*

48. You've been working toward this moment since you heard that really motivational song last week. = *-3 points*

49. You've spent the last few months "practicing excellence" at your day job, which will serve you well when you pursue your dream more fully. = *+2 points*

50. You've spent the last few months cultivating bitterness and your exit will be met with cheers. = *-10 points*

51. You're trying to pursue someone else's dream, (your mother's, a teacher's, a friend's, etc.) instead of your own. = *-3 points*

52. You saw the length of this scorecard and thought, *That is so long and feels like hard work. I don't like hard work, I just want to dream! Dream, I tell you!* = *-3 points*

Totals:

Fewer than 0 points – 10 points: Job Lover or Serial Quitter
If you managed to score negatively on this quiz, one of two things is going on: You love your job and are right where you need to be. Or you are a serial quitter and hate your job so much you haven't had a chance to love your dream. To the first person, I'd like to say, "Bravo," but that sounds borderline like the friend you have who says "Ciao" all the time, despite being from Ohio. So instead, I say, "Congrats." You've got a job you love that loves you back and is structured in a way that allows you to work equally hard at both your day job and your dream. Or your job is already your dream. That's great; not everyone on the planet needs to quit their day job. My friend Bob uses his job as a lawyer, which he loves, to fund missions around the

world (which he loves even more). He (and you) are rare but awesome. To the serial quitter I'd say, "Push pause." Your dissatisfaction might have clouded your vision to such a degree that if you quit right now, you'd just land at another job you eventually hate and start the cycle all over again without making any progress on your dream. Don't quit right now. Reread the "Don't Quit Your Job" chapter.

11–30 points: Stirred Up

Something is afoot. You've bumped into something that made you feel alive. Your dream is starting to percolate and you've started to see that maybe what you're currently doing isn't what you really want to be doing forty hours a week. You finished this book and were confronted with a lot of questions. "Could I really do this? What do I really want to do? Am I hustling right now on the things that matter?" You're not ready to quit your day job right this second, but you may have taken the first step toward a completely new adventure that will unfold over the next few years.

31–50 points: One Foot Out The Door

You took notes in this book. Not just with a pen, but with several different highlighters and a key to explain what each color means. You might have even purchased a case of this book and handed it out to all your friends, which I really appreciate. You've made some plans. You've worked on your dream job. You've got a few pieces in place. There are still a few that elude you though. You don't have a "big next thing" lined up. Maybe your emergency fund could be bigger. You could spend a little more time practicing excellence at your job. As annoying as it is, this might be one of those moments like the one in *Braveheart* where William Wallace yells, "Hold! Hold!" to his men as they crouch waiting for England's horses to barrel down on them. They want to stand, they are desperate to stand, but to do so too early would be disastrous. I encourage you to hold right now and get your final pieces in place before you quit. The exciting thing is that it might be a matter of months before you quit, not years.

More than 50 points: It's Go Time

I'm not sure what you're waiting for. You've got a huge new dream-scented opportunity on the table. You're financially prepared. Your spouse or family is on board. You've spent the last few months, if not years, falling in like with your day job while you worked on something on the side that you love. There's a window that is closing and if you miss it, it might not come around again for a long time. You've assessed all the risks and are making a decision that is motivated in wise hope, not nervous fear. It's go time. Quit already. Kick rocks. Live your dream.

Now clearly, that list was scientific. Depending on your score, you are 100 percent guaranteed to have the results I described, and if things don't work out when you quit, you should send me hate mail and feign great surprise that a scorecard that contains the word *booty* led you astray. Obviously, there's no such thing as a periodic table of elements for quitting. That scorecard gives you an idea, but what are the other ways you'll know if you're ready to quit? How did I know when it was time to quit?

Six reasons I quit my last job

Dave Ramsey approached me about working with him in June 2010. By the first week of August, we had moved from Atlanta, found a new school for my oldest daughter, and rented a house in Nashville. But that whole experience started with me quitting my job. Which as I've mentioned a number of times, I am awesome at.

This time was different though. I've always traded an old day job for a new day job. I've always left one situation I didn't love for another I thought would be different but ultimately never was. So why in a period of eight weeks did my wife and I make that decision? How did I know it was time to quit my day job and pursue my dream job?

1. **We had somewhere to land.**

   Just like in the rest of the book, the specifics of your situation are going to be different from mine, but the principles still hold. Whether you're breeding chinchillas or starting a nonprofit that fights against businesses that breed chinchillas ("Soft Coats Are Rough on Chinchillas, Inc.") you can apply these ideas to a host of dreams.

   For two years, my wife and I talked about my quitting my job at AutoTrader.com. Our conversation intensified in some seasons and dissipated in others, but quitting has been a constant undercurrent to my work experience for most of my life. However, this was the first time in my twelve-year career that I had somewhere to land that fit within my long-term goals of being an author and a speaker. This was the first time I wasn't just trading out a Granny Smith apple for a Fuji. Although I would have the security and community of being at a full-time job in an office environment, this would be unlike anything I'd ever done before. I wasn't just trading out my old day job, which I had grown to really like, for another. I was jumping to what felt like the right opportunity.

Your dream might not be another job. It might be a chance to serve in a country you feel called to. You might get a long-term freelance contract that allows you to string together a year of work in the field you really love. Someone may place an order for a million chinchillas.

When this happens, you have to be honest about whether you have somewhere real to land. Somewhere that will actually support your long-term goals. Sometimes the situation doesn't present itself as an opportunity that will line up perfectly with your dreams. Sometimes it will just be a much higher percentage of dream time than you currently have now.

Will the new opportunity offer you a larger percentage of time to focus on your dream? If your current job only offers you weekends, mornings and evenings to work on your dream, will the new job offer you a lot more time? Could you work four days in the office and one day on your dream?

The percent has to be dramatic because otherwise the risk isn't worth it. If your current job offers you thirty minutes at lunch to do your thing and a potential new job would offer you forty-five minutes, it's not worth disrupting your entire life.

I faced that situation the summer we decided to work for Dave Ramsey.

A multibillion-dollar company had an ad agency that offered me a job. I'd be well paid, have unique opportunities to work on interesting advertising projects and only do four days of work a week. In addition to all the other perks, I had the chance to actually spend part of my workweek on my own dream. That felt like a dramatic difference to me. I would have taken it because they offered me more dream time than AutoTrader.com did. But the Dave Ramsey job offered me a far larger percentage of time each week to do the things I loved. There were certainly other factors involved in my decision, but the percentage of dream time is a good measurement to begin with when it comes to determining somewhere stable to land.

2. The opportunity fit our opportunity filter.

Years before Dave Ramsey offered me a job, my wife and I discussed the filter we would use to find a dream job. When StuffChristiansLike.net took off, we had an inclination that AutoTrader.com might not be my career's final resting place.

So we started discussing what criteria the next opportunity needed to fit. This was helpful because it took the pressure off of looking for the perfect job—which is the equivalent of trying to find one needle out of a country-sized haystack—and instead allowed us to brainstorm the characteristics my dream job might possess.

We both felt it should be at a company where faith was part of the culture, not just something that happened in pockets.

I didn't want to work at a church. I've freelanced for churches for years. I have friends who love their jobs at churches across the country. My dad's a pastor and it would be easy to think I need to follow in his footsteps. But I never felt as if a church was where I was called to be.

I wanted to work in a team environment where I was surrounded by people all day. As a writer, I've never been great at the Stephen King, sit-in-a-cabin-in-Maine-alone-for-three-months-writing-a-book gig. (That's only one of the characteristics that differentiates the two of us; the millions of books he's sold is the other.)

I wanted to work at a company where an individual had grown a personal brand successfully and humbly, without getting lost in all the traps that face leaders.

Location was a factor!

I wanted to stay in the Southeast. Although I grew up in Massachusetts, the South was now my home. As we started to discuss these factors, an activity that happened mostly in those Adirondack chairs in our side yard, we started to eliminate a lot of companies. We had that filter in place, and when the Dave Ramsey opportunity came up, we checked it against our criteria.

Faith is a big part of the culture at Dave Ramsey, so that one passed the test. It wasn't a church, but it was actually a for-profit business actively involved in the marketplace. They had a staff of 300 people I'd get to interact with. I could still write and speak without doing a one-man show from my basement. And I'd be based out of Nashville, which was perfect, geographically speaking. Dave has also spent seventeen years growing a personal brand. He's got a huge radio audience, is a *New York Times* best-selling author, and has spoken to hundreds of thousands of people. And he's managed to not become a jerk along the way. That's no easy feat.

One by one, our filter criteria were met, which helped us feel good about the decision to quit. It's important to note that the level of detail you put in your own opportunity filter will vary by item. For instance, some of them will be specific and measurable, like, "We don't want to work at a church." That one was easy to verify and check off. Others will be broader and less defined, like, "Be at a company where faith is part of the culture." That's more difficult to measure. So as you build your filter, try to have a mix of both the specific and the broad.

3. We tested the dream before we quit.

Although I didn't talk to Dave about a job until June 2010, I started talking with his team about working there in 2008. That was the year I came up and spoke to his entire team one morning. It was an amazing experience and as I mentioned before, I thought to myself, *This is it!* I called my wife and told her we were moving to Nashville because I was definitely going to take a job with Dave Ramsey's team!

It turns out the job I was offered was the wrong fit in the right company. Then I talked to the head of publishing there about a different job. That one had the word *coordinator* in the title, which means I would have radically failed at it. So I told them that would be a horrible fit. A year later they invited me back to speak again. The event went well and once again I drove back to Atlanta, having enjoyed the experience but not certain I would ever work there.

A year after that, they invited me up for a third time to speak, and that's when Dave pulled me aside with the job idea.

When we were offered the job, we had already spent two years testing the waters before we quit. I'd spoken there three times, met dozens of people I'd be working with and got a sense of the culture. "Practicing" the dream helped me feel good about committing to it.

It's like working weekends on a local farm before you start your own. Or designing free Christmas cards for all your friends before you open your own freelance design studio. When my dream job came along, it wasn't a day-one decision; it was a year-two decision. Whenever possible, before you quit make a point of practicing what you want to do with your life.

4. **We had a support network.**

I think dreaming works best as a team sport. In order to grow your dream as fast and as far as it can possibly grow, you need people who will support you every step along the way. They might not be as passionate as you are for your dream. They might not feel the same degree of fire you feel, but you need people who in a variety of ways are on your side. Looking at our decision to move to Nashville and join Dave Ramsey, my wife and I knew we had that.

I spoke in depth with both my parents and my wife's parents. As a pastor, my dad has God's direct line. It's like the red bat phone, which is nice, so I had that going for me. Okay, that's not true. But having stepped out of everything he knew in North Carolina with three young kids to move to Massachusetts in the 80s to start a church, he and my mom understand what it means to take risks. My father-in-law helps lead one of the largest home-building companies in the country, so from a business perspective he was able to help me think through many of the specific challenges ahead with quitting my stable job. They asked questions, they poked and prodded, but above all they supported us. We didn't feel it was "us against the world." It was a good feeling. Granted, we were fortunate to not have crazy parents. If yours fall into that category, disregard everything they say and don't eat the homemade desserts they mail you. The post office is not a magical refrigeration device. That cake is going to be disgusting.

One of my younger brothers, Will, also lives in Nashville with his wife, Tiffany. Every time I came to visit I would stay with them. I loved the idea of being in the same city as my brother and having our wives become better friends.

I also had friendships with a few people I'd seen around the conference circuit. (It's not really a circuit so much as it is a loop, but circuit sounds like we make more money than we really do, so let's go with that.) I knew that in Nashville I could connect with my friends, plug into a church, and have a sense of community even though we'd never lived there.

Last, but certainly not least, I had the support of the people who read my blog. I know I might never meet most of them face to face. I know that we might not recognize each other on the street. But readers of the blog have been exposed to and helped shape my dream job for years. From the moment I launched the site, I had interaction and encouragement from them. When I do something that feels out of step with the expectations I've set with my writing, they are quick to let me know. Not all of them are concerned about my well-being. One reader suggested I kill myself. A handful of others said I am in fact a horrible person. But the vast majority of my blog readers provide a unique chance for me to say to a group of people, "I'm going on an adventure; want to come with me?"

The day I announced we had moved to Nashville was one of the biggest traffic days in the blog's history as hundreds of supportive comments and emails flooded in. The blog was a big part of the reason I was able to even have a shot at my dream, and therefore, it only made sense to include those readers in my support network.

5. **We were stupid rich.**

Not really. We were ballin' on a budget, sitting on whatever size rims a used Sequoia with a third-row seat offers, and checking books out of the library. But we had the money to move and jump to a new job that wouldn't initially pay as well as my old one.

We could afford to move. We could pay to put new carpet in our Atlanta home to replace the muted green look the lady before us chose. We could afford to have the entire interior painted so we could sell the house in the middle of a horrible economy. We could afford the first month's rent and security deposit on a rental house in Nashville. We could afford three months of temporary health insurance while we waited for my 90-day probationary period to be over.

We could do all those things and many more that often come with a big dream and a big move, because we had our finances in order. How? Two things really. The first is that I hustled on freelance gigs and we had the patience to pay off our bills. We wanted money to fund our dreams, not limit them, and we worked hard to financially remove things that stood in the way. The second big thing was that in 2004, years before I worked for Dave Ramsey, we read his book *The Total Money Makeover*. That book dramatically changed the way we looked at money and, unbeknownst to us at the time, allowed us to financially follow our dream years later. Clearly I'm biased about that book, but I don't get any money for recommending it. If I did, I would have mentioned it a few thousand times already and probably had the title sewn into my pants like NASCAR. Nonetheless I assure you it's a great read and can play a big role in dream pursuit.

6. God seemed cool with it.

Although God is the wild card and can certainly call you on adventures you can't ignore, we didn't get any handwriting on the wall. I have yet to converse with a burning bush. No prophetic donkeys crossed our paths as we weighed out our decision to leave Atlanta. But through praying and spending a lot of time wrestling with God on this decision, we felt like this jump was where he was calling us.

We didn't try to force God's hand or do the "I just heard a sermon about David and Goliath so I need to quit my job right this second" leap of faith that's so popular in Christian circles. We took our time with the decision, like another guy in the Bible, named Jesus. He spent thirty years in obscurity before he started his adventure. Often, we're not willing to spend thirty minutes in preparation, never mind thirty years, especially when we come home from a conference and find our day jobs waiting for us on Monday morning. I'm not sure why Christians sometimes think the maturation of our own missions will be radically shorter than that of Jesus. But it happens and in the past I've certainly wanted to take wild, unplanned, possibly-not-inspired-by-God leaps of faith.

Those are the six reasons we felt it would be good to quit my job. Ultimately, we realized that passing up this opportunity would cost us more than taking it. Still, there are two things I wish we had done that might have made the first six months a lot easier.

Rules

My wife was standing in the laundry room, crying. My first inclination was to think this was due to the difficulty of folding clothes for little kids. All those socks, those miniature sweaters and pants the size of potato chip bags. Anyone can fold a load of towels. It takes like three folds. Thirty seconds, tops. But kids' clothes multiply like rabbits when you put them in the dryer. A single laundry basket can hold hundreds of items. It can be very demoralizing.

That was not why she was crying.

She was crying because I was out of town seven out of eight weekends after moving to Nashville. During my three years at AutoTrader.com I was never once out of town for business. I used to get home every day at 4:30 in the afternoon. Now, in what was billed as my "dream job," I was gone all the time.

I felt unmoored from my family, as if I was not anchored in the same place they were but was out floating somewhere. My wife felt disconnected from me and my kids hadn't seen me in so long that they started calling me "Denny" instead of "Daddy." It was a bad scene.

How did this happen?

We never talked about the rules. In the shadow of the overwhelming opportunity, we forget to establish some new rules for this new life of ours.

We never sat down and said, "Let's look at the calendar and make sure you're not on the road back-to-back weekends if at all possible. Let's block out weekends in busy speaking months so that the speakers group knows not to book you then. Let's make a rule that we won't go X number of weekends without the family doing a big family event that doesn't involve the Wii."

We came into the situation big on excitement and small on strategy. So when my team leader asked me to speak at all of the Dave Ramsey live events to thousands of people, I was thrilled at that opportunity and said yes! But I already had a fall's worth of my own events booked before I started my new job. My events plus Dave's events collided, creating situations where I was all over the place and constantly out of town.

One weekend I flew to San Diego from Nashville. I spoke at eight in the morning and jumped on a flight through Phoenix and Las Vegas before landing in Orlando at midnight. Saturday morning I spoke at one of Dave's events and then flew back to Nashville that night.

After stringing a few events like that together, my family was ready to kill me. And they had every right to, especially since I could have mitigated this by having some pre-established rules. For instance, if one of our rules had been no back-to-back weekends, then I could have discussed that with my team leader when the possible collisions occurred. (Months after that bad stretch, I talked to him and he implored me to let him know about things like that because that was neither his intent nor the heart of the company.)

So if you do quit your day job for a dream job, try your best to have some pre-established ground rules to live by. You don't have to be married to make the commitment in the same way you don't need to be married to go on a diet. Think ahead to what you're planning to do and make some rules then. It's so much harder to do this when you're in the trenches. You'll cave in a lot faster too if your list is just loosely stored in your head or your heart, quite possibly the worst place to store something other than undying love and your feelings for Nutella.

Write down some rules. They're going to change; they're going to grow; they'll even be a little flexible. During the release of this book, I will hopefully be on the road doing a book tour, which will mean more travel time than every other month of the year, for instance. But once you've got your rules written down, share them with someone who will hold you accountable to them.

Risk list

My wife is sitting on our couch, crying. Not really, but that last section felt so emotionally charged I thought I would try to keep the vibe going. She wasn't really crying, but she was sweaty nervous. (Thus far, I've described my wife as "crying" and "sweaty." Great husband. I assure you that she is double *t* hott and wicked smart and the best thing that ever happened to me.)

We were talking about a mortgage on a house we were looking at. For some reason, buying a house in Franklin, Tennessee, was proving to be more difficult than selling our house in Atlanta. Our first offer on a house fell through. Our second offer on a different house fell through. Our third offer on a third house fell through. And each week closer to our one-year rental agreement being over, we got more nervous. It was easy to look for houses in the fall, but once we hit February and still didn't have a house, the end of our rental in July started racing to-ward us. With each month that passed, we knew we'd have to lower our standards and buy a house we might not love. We decided to name all the months. We called February "February Fun," because we still felt we had time to get a house we really liked. We named March "March Madness," because we'd probably have to buy a house we just kind of liked. We decided after that we'd have "April Angst," being forced to get a house we kind of disliked. May we just called "Mayhem," because if we weren't in a house by then, all sorts of nonsense must have broken out.

Part of the pressure we faced was that in addition to there only being three houses for sale in Tennessee, I was also on a commission/salary mix for the first time in my life. The pressure of that was starting to get a little terrifying. Book sales were no longer gravy; they were the meat and potatoes too. Advertising on my blog was no longer extra money with which we could enjoy cash pillow fights in the front yard.

We started having money conversations we never had when I was at AutoTrader.com. That job wasn't risky. It was steady and consistent, like a delightful geyser I couldn't get the copyright to mention by name in this book. The checks just came, right on time. Sure, it was subject to the whims of the economy, but barring massive layoffs, I knew I had a paycheck of the same size every two weeks.

Now the punctuation in our life had changed when it came to the money we had. Some months it would be an exclamation mark. "Look at the commission we got on the book sales!" Other months it would be a question mark. "We got our paycheck and the commissions are down. Which area do we need to be extra careful on this month?"

Whether or not those fears would come to fruition didn't matter in that moment; they were what we felt. And despite the support network I mentioned earlier, we felt alone with a lot of these risks. We had relationships that were woven over a period of six years in Atlanta. You can't fast-forward something like that in a new town.

It was a season of doubt and sleepless nights. And looking back, I believe a lot of it could have been reduced if we had made a "risk list."

A risk list is exactly what it sounds like, a list of risks. (Brilliant, right? That's why they wanted to put me on the cover with the arm-fold-of-confidence pose. I wouldn't let them, though, because I'm humble.)

Before you quit your day job and pursue your dream job in a full-time capacity, make a list of all the risks that might come up. There will be some you don't see, but it's not difficult to brainstorm a few. Here is what our risk list might have looked like before we moved to Nashville:

Friendships

Jenny will be leaving a group of girls she's been meeting with for three years and knows like sisters. Jon will be at work, surrounded all day by people, so he won't naturally feel as friendless as Jenny. Friendships taking a long time to form in Nashville is a risk.

Travel

If speaking offers go as well as possible, Jon will be out of town more often, at a time when the kids will be in a new city with new schools and will really need their dad around.

Money

Websites fall out of favor in the blink of an eye. Ask My-Space or Friendster. If the traffic to StuffChristiansLike.net tanks and advertisers pull out, we will lose a significant portion of our ability to pay our bills.

House

We can't buy a house until we sell our house in Atlanta. We'll have to rent a house. That means for at least a few months, we'll be carrying a mortgage and a rent bill at the same time. That's a huge financial risk.

And so forth. That's what we should have done. We didn't. It ended up amplifying the stress when we actually dealt with those risks. You can't imagine how much better you feel when you can go back to a journal or a whiteboard,

The Three Reasons You'll Ignore Everything You Just Read

When I started writing this book, I asked people on my blog to send me their ideas about the "I'm, but" equation. For example, "I'm a teacher, but I want to be an artist." I essentially asked, "Have you ever felt trapped between the tension of a day job and a dream job?" I expected to get three or four dozen responses because it was during the holidays, and I thought this might not be an issue everyone dealt with.

More than 600 people responded.

Some of them were lighthearted. "I am a record-keeping and reporting specialist, but my dream since twelve was to be in the WWE. Far cry, I know."

Some of them were sad. "I tried to send something last night, but I just cried instead. Maybe I'll try again in a day or so."

With hundreds of responses you're bound to have a unique mix of people say a unique mix of things. But in reading through them and the comments on my blog, there were a handful of fairly consistent objections that emerged.

Rather than dance around them or slowly unpack them, a word I learned from my counselor, I thought it would be better to just throw them on the table. Because, more than just objections, I think these are the three reasons you'll ignore everything you just read in this book.

1. **You think life exists outside your four office walls**.
This is easily the most common objection to all the content in this book. The theory is basically that you can turn yourself off when you go home. You can "leave work at work" and enjoy your "real life." This is a fun thing to tell yourself and I've said it hundreds of times myself. When my blog started gaining momentum in 2008 I distinctly remember thinking, *My blog, my personal writing, my family, my church, those are the things that constitute my life. This is just my day job.*

This is a particularly deceptive thing to think because it starts off from a good place. I don't want to be obsessed with work when I get home. I want my family to feel like I am present. In the middle of dinner my wife has said to me before, "Where are you right now?" She said that because I was not mentally present at home; I was still at the office. So the ability to leave work at work is a good thing. But when we take that ability to the extreme, we end up thinking that we can really have two different versions of ourselves, "work me" and "life me." We believe we can separate the two cleanly with some mental razorblade. We can't.

You can't spend forty hours a week doing something and think it won't impact you.

You can't spend half of your waking hours somewhere and think it doesn't affect you.

You can't make a perfectly clean break between your life inside and outside work.

If you've ever been chewed out at work, I promise you didn't forget about that the minute you were off the clock. If your girlfriend broke up with you or your husband cheated on you, you didn't spend forty happy hours at work because that bad stuff happened outside your work life. You are one person, you're messy and you tend to spill work into home and home into work.

When you think about it, the "it's just a job" belief is crazy. Imagine telling a friend, "I have to go somewhere five days a week, dedicate the majority of my waking hours to it, let it control my vacation and travel plans and let it be the sole provider for my lifestyle. But I don't consider it part of my life." That friend would think you're out of your mind. Not only is it part of your life; it's dictating a large part of it.

A variation of this belief is the equally popular "My career doesn't define me" approach. Another way to say it is, "Work is what I do, not who I am. I do accounting, I'm not an accountant." I agree, sort of. While I agree that your job isn't your identity, while I agree your whole life is not represented by your job title, it does indeed define you.

Be honest and say what you really mean: "My current career doesn't define me."

If you had the job you really wanted, you'd love to have that be part of your identity. If you were a painter, you wouldn't say, "I'm not an artist; I create art." You'd love to tell people, "I'm an artist!" And whenever a musician is interviewed you'll hear this approach slip out: "Well, as a musician, it's important to me that the sound of the album have a certain feel." And I'm not immune to that either. When I finally published a book, I couldn't wait to say, "I'm an author. I'm an author!" When I had lunch with my oldest daughter at her school and she told her classmates, "My dad is an author," I was thrilled.

That was a label I wanted to spoon at night and couple skate with at Roller Kingdom. I was more than happy that the word *author* was added to the definition of who I was. Was it the completion or the entirety of my existence? Not at all. But to say that being an author didn't define me, at least in healthy ways, would have been a lie.

Plus, if you truly believe your life exists outside of work, that your job doesn't define you, what do we call those forty hours? Death? Weekly purgatory?

If you come in each morning with the attitude that you have to shut your life off and spend eight hours not living, how do you think you'll actually perform? It always comes down to this eventually. You can fake it for months, maybe even years, convincing everyone you work with that you care about the company, the business or the job. But your apathy for a job always comes out eventually.

And when it does you have three options. You can admit to your coworkers that the job isn't really your life. Some of them will understand, especially if you're working retail. But some of your coworkers will be extremely insulted to hear you say, "This is just a job; this isn't my life." Some of them put passion and heart into what they do and will hear, correctly or incorrectly, that you hate that job and think anyone who loves that job is ignorant.

Your second option is to just be a jerk. I've spent a lot of years pursuing the finer points of this particular approach. I was a bit of a punk in high school, but I really came into my own as an adult. I think being a jerk is ultimately why I got fired from my second job and essentially run out of the building at my seventh. I checked out of the seventh one about three months before I actually quit. My two weeks' notice was supposed to be up on a Friday, but I was such a jerk that my boss asked me to leave abruptly in the middle of the day on Wednesday. I began clearing out my desk. Thirty minutes later my boss stood up in her cubicle next to mine and asked, "What is taking so long, Jon? Just go." I think they probably would have gotten a security guard to toss me out on the street like a drunk contestant on *The Bachelorette* but our building didn't have one.

The few remaining friends I had at that company emailed me days later and said, "Why didn't you come say goodbye before you left?" I didn't know what to say.

Writing those paragraphs made me feel a little sick to my stomach. But that's the kind of thing that can happen when you try to live your entire life outside of work. I don't think you'll ever become as big a jerk as I can be. I'm special. But honestly tell me if you think a manager at a company has ever said, "You know when Mark became a great employee? Someone who is just an amazingly high performer? You know when that happened? When he recognized that this job is just a job and his real life is outside of these walls." No one will ever say that because it's next to impossible, and it's also a fairly poor way to impress the boss.

So your first two options when you get tired of pretending to be happy or fulfilled or engaged at work are to: 1) admit to all your coworkers you don't think your job matters or, 2) become a jerk.

Neither is particularly fun, but there is a third option. Don't quit right away. If you quit your job without understanding why you're quitting, you'll just jump from job to job to job. You'll become a serial quitter like I was. The things you didn't like at the job before will show up in your next job. And the next. The common denominator in every bad job you've quit is you. That's why this third option is so significant. If you choose to not quit right away, you can begin closing the gap between your day job and your dream job. It's challenging, certainly, but it's completely possible and it's what this book was all about.

2. **You think your job just funds the rest of your life.**
Again, this one is almost right, which makes sense. If these objections were obvious and neon, we could all just dismiss them and get on with doing what we love with our lives.

This argument is essentially the "my life is outside my job," only now we've thrown money into the equation. You've still got all the potential dangers that come with going to work with your body but not your heart. Now you're going to work primarily for your wallet. The funny thing is that we hate this approach when we see it in other types of people.

My friends can't stand the NBA because it's all just some spoiled athletes who don't really care about their city or their team now. Gone are the days when being a Celtic or a Laker meant something, when Larry Bird or Magic Johnson carried the hopes of an entire state into the championship. Sportscasters and coaches have long bemoaned the fact that in college, athletes play for the name on the front of the jersey; in the pros, they play for the name on the back of the jersey. It's like their job funds the rest of their life.

Same with musicians or bands. When someone gets popular or a band lets one of their songs be used in a car commercial their fans don't like, people are quick to call them "sellouts." They're just doing it for the money now. It used to be about the music. Of course, the guitar player who practices nonstop and tours 200 days a year would probably call that "work." But that's beside the point. They've lost their integrity. It's almost like their job just funds the rest of their life.

You're not a musician. You're not a basketball player, fine. Neither am I. I actually played a total of sixty-eight seconds during my entire eighth grade season. I was the skinny white kid everyone hoped would hit a basket in the final four seconds of every home game. But you don't have to be a basketball player or a bass player to see that the phrase "My job just funds the rest of my life" is no way to go through life. I don't want us prostituting ourselves for forty hours a week. I also don't want to pretend that there won't be jobs or seasons when it will be primarily just about making the ends meet. I'm not going to glamorize a ditch-digging job—even at my dream job right now there are tasks I do to fund other things.

But I do want to rewrite that idea. I don't think we should say: "My job just funds the rest of my life." I think we should say: "My job funds my dreams."

The word *just* strips away every other benefit of your job, leaving you only the money. Social interaction, the chance to do something that matters to someone, the simple act of accomplishing something, the chance to practice some aspect of your dream, we lose sight of all those things when we are obsessed with "just funds."

I don't like "the rest of my life" because it sounds like life only occurs outside of the job, and we know that is not true. I'd much rather us be deliberate about using our day jobs as "fundraising" for our dream jobs. I don't think there's anything wrong with saying, "I'm a doctor. I have a thriving practice and the money I make from that allows me to do huge things in the lives of people around me. I can build wells and hospitals and a million other things because I'm faithful to my day job." What I don't want to happen is to have your job just fund your life without ever thinking about or working on your dream job. I don't want you to wake up at sixty-five and realize, "I spent forty of my best years doing something that just funded my life."

3. **You think work is never meant to be fulfilling.**
    "Part of growing up is on some sad level accepting the math of the world. Meaning we end up, for the most part, working to make ends meet rather than working to fulfill dreams." That is what one person told me. Another said, "People just need to put things in perspective and realize that there is no golden cure to all of life's ailments."

    Those are depressing statements perhaps, but there is truth to them. We do need to make ends meet. We do have bills to pay and despite the sheer amount of awesomeness I have tried to pack into this book, I fear you did not find a golden cure to all of life's ailments in it.

But who says following a dream is about having fun all the time? I didn't. Doing work you love is not about doing work that is fun all the time or even feels good all the time. Regardless of your dream, there are going to be hard moments. You'll have to do things you don't necessarily enjoy or don't necessarily have an easy time doing. Anyone who tells you otherwise must have access to a magical unicorn named Cornelius who grants wishes with his tears.

The danger in this type of thinking is that it dresses itself up like hard work or a can-do attitude but often it's just a fancy way of hiding fear. The reason is that there's finality to this logic. The unspoken ending when someone says, "Who says work has to be fun all the time?" is, "so let's not try to change it at all."

No one thinks, *Who says work has to be fun all the time? But I bet we can make it fun some of the time!* But someone should. Okay, I will.

Ultimately, I agree that work will not be fun all the time. But I don't want work to be fun all the time. I want it to have meaning all the time. Even if you're doing a menial task that is way beneath you, I want it to have meaning.

"The least of things with a meaning," said the famed Swiss psychologist Carl Jung, "is worth more in life than the greatest of things without it."[19]

I know sometimes our day jobs feel meaningless. But they're always a great place to start dreaming. They're also a great place to start changing the world.

That's what happened to me when I finally got serious about closing the gap between my day job and my dream job. In the middle of one of the worst economies in recent history. In the middle of a day job with busy work and paperwork and corporate memos. In the middle of knowing, "This can't be what I do for the rest of my life," I changed the world. I partnered with the readers of Stuff Christians Like and we raised $60,000 in twenty-five days to build two kindergartens in Vietnam.

And it all started from a cubicle. It all started in the tension between a day job and a dream job. I didn't quit my job so I could move to Costa Rica on friends' and family's dime. I didn't eat, pray, love my way around the globe. I had a part-time dream and a full-time day job. And if you do too, I promise that's more than enough to begin doing something truly meaningful. Do it wisely and it will grow from there.

Start where you are. Start with what you have. Start today.

Sources

1. A 2010 survey conducted by job placement firm Manpower.
2. http://www.bls.gov/news.release/tenure.t01.htm, March 28, 2011.
3. Mario Testino, "How to Look Like a Movie Star." *GQ*, January 2011, 53.
4. http://thinkexist.com/quotes/henry_hartman/, March 28, 2011.
5. Simon Sinek, *Start with Why* (Portfolio, 2009).
6. The Leadership Summit, 2006, Willow Creek Church.
7. Gordon MacKenzie, *Orbiting the Giant Hairball* (Viking, 1998),19–20.
8. *The Talented Mr. Ripley*, Paramount Pictures, 1999.
9. Julie B. Shor, *The Overworked American* (Basic Books, 1993), from the publisher's Amazon.com description.
10. Michael J. Gelb, *How to Think Like Leonardo da Vinci* (Dell, 2000), 23.
11. While speaking at the Catalyst Conference, Atlanta, October 8, 2009.
12. Seth Godin, *The Dip* (Portfolio Hardover, 2007), 68.
13. *Spin*, August 2010, 58.
14. While speaking at the Catalyst Conference, Atlanta, October 8, 2009.
15. *Rolling Stone*, Issue 1122, January 20, 2011, 46.
16. Pat Riley, *Show Time* (Grand Central Publishing, 1988).
17. Cameron Stauth, *The Franchise* (William Morrow & Co, 1990), 310, 311.
18. *Vanity Fair*, February 2011, 159.
19. http://thinkexist.com/quotations/meaning/, March 28, 2011.

Acknowledgments

First and foremost, I want to thank God. Not in a "mandatory religious shout-out" way, but more in a "reason I breathe, source of all my hope, cause of all my dreams" kind of way.

Jenny Acuff, my beautiful wife. Thanks for dreaming big and loud with me. Without your constant love and wisdom this book would never exist. I love you. L.E. and McRae, I can't wait to see what your dreams are. I promise to do everything I can as a proud dad to help you accomplish them. Mom and Dad. Will, Tiffany, Bennett, Sally, Mac and Molly Acuff. John and Laura Calbert. Marci and Justin Saknini.

Dave Ramsey and Bill Hampton, thank you for bringing me to Lampo. Your leadership is a constant gift and your support of this book continues to overwhelm me. Preston Cannon for shepherding *Quitter* from idea to final book. Daniel Bell, Jen Sievertsen, Kelli Hansbauer, Katie Crenshaw, Ben Lalisan, Brian Williams, Hannah Cook, Shane Helm, Darcie Clemen, Andrew Kallemeyn, Erin McAtee, Dino Evangelista, Jeremy Shearer, Bobby Marko, Collin Fatke, Neal Webb, Jeremy Breland, Liz Edwards,

Beth Tallent, Chris Mefford, Mike Pappas, Mindy Shipley, Brett Kozimor, Jake Isham, Cam Cornelius, Meg Hill, Dave Oglesby, Jess Sloan, Diana Key, Josh Holloway, Steve NeSmith, Tim Walsh and the entire team at Dave Ramsey for their massive help and creativity.

Brent Cole, your brilliant input as an editor was critical to this book. Mrs. Harris, Chris Thomas, Stephen Rose, Grant Jenkins, Stephen Brewster, Mike Foster, Al Andrews, Donald Miller, Bob Goff (for the great 800-number idea and nonstop inspiration), Holly Justice and the team at AutoTrader.com. Mike, Lynn, Wendy and Erin Maybury. Explosions in the Sky, Ben Arment, Brad Lomenick, Tim Sanders, Pete Wilson, Carlos Whittaker, Steven Pressfield and Anne Lamott.

And all the readers of StuffChristiansLike.net. Your generosity is the reason I get to write books and encourage people from stage and do a million other fun things.

Thank you.

The Quitter 100,

a group of people who generously volunteered to read the manuscript of this book and provided invaluable feedback.

Lauren Childers
Andrea Saffle
Gerri Jackson
Dustin Grant
Gregory Sharp
Jordan Watson
Ty Cedars
Brian Adams
Becky Miller
Jessica Peterman
Ashley Burgamy
Hilary L. Hymer
Jenni Meyers
Jared Massey
Lindsey Harris
Shannah Hayley
Curtis Honeycutt
Janelle Keith
Howard Fryberger
Patrick Serban
Michael Ulrich
Ben Meredith
Renda Olson
Barbie de la Torre
Shelle Lenssen
Elisa Handley
Ami McCain
Phil Hoover
Michelle Woodman
James Pomeroy
Niki Gray
Cristin Henry
Destiny Riggleman
Ken Guie

Ben Atkinson
Amber Humphries
Lindsey Allen
Rachel Porter
Chuck L Baker
Beth Quarles
Milanne Pizarro
Anne Verrastro
Cristopher Thomas
Jacqueline Hernandez
Brenda Patik
Natalie Duncan
Melissa Couch
Jeannie Naylor
Brad Keller
Adam Bright
Amy Hinds
Ken Saxton
Kelly Levatino
Jessa Stave
Ricky Anderson
Zechariah Brewer
BJ Smith
Karyn Craft
Ryan Kennedy
Micah Drushal
Jenna Benton
Peter Adams
Seth Fendley
David Bouchard
Michelle Pulido
Heather Vires
David Tate
Brandy Bordner

Michelle Hurst
Chris Sernel
Katie McNemar
Gina Darby
Robin Case
Mariah Coronado
Megan Watson
Tom Branch Jr
Karen Koch
Jeff Childs
Mike Levy
Beth Lazear
Brittany Dowdy
Chris Snyder
Curtis DuMont
Tyson Ramsdell
Brian Hunteman
Wayne Franklin
Kyle Clark
Victoria Andrews
Aaron Matthews
Chuck Gray
Kimberly Arrowood
Nancy Goedhart
Heidi Dieckmann
Viq Thomasson
Kathy McFeeters
Nina Rogers
Leanne Little
Lauren Thacker
Charles Vanderford
Nic Casey

WHAT'S YOUR DREAM?

What's something that makes you feel alive that you wish you were doing?

What do you hope is true of your life in six months? A year? Three years?

Sometimes, the first step to closing the gap between your day job and your dream job is to answer those questions honestly, out loud, to yourself.

I want to give you a place to do that, so I created a toll-free number you can call.

When you call it, you'll hear a message from me and can then leave a message for yourself. I'll never share or sell your number. I won't email you the message or make you check back on it ever again. This is just your chance to tell yourself out loud about the you, you'd like to be.

Here's the number. I hope to hear from you soon and often.

888.406.7640

Continue The Conversation

BLOG

Get more ideas about what it means to be a Quitter, meet other people who are working on their dreams, and continue closing the gap between your day job and your dream job at Jon's blog: jonacuff.com

TWITTER

@jonacuff

FACEBOOK

www.facebook.com/quitterbook
www.facebook.com/authorjonacuff

SPEAKING

Hear Jon live at one of his speaking engagements or book him for your event: jonacuff.com/speaking

QUESTIONS & FEEDBACK

quitter@quitterbook.com

5 Questions to Ask a Hinge Moment

1. Do I love doing _____ enough to do it for free?

2. When I _____ does time feel different?

3. Do I enjoy doing _____ regardless of the opinions of other people?

4. If I pursue _____ and only my life changes, is that enough?

5. Is this the first time I've loved _____ or is this part of a bigger pattern in my life?

5 Reasons I Work Right Now

My Like vs. Love List

My Risk List

SCHEDULE JONACUFF FOR YOUR NEXT EVENT!

Visit **daveramsey.com/speakers**
or call **888.284.2488**